Jonathan Edwards on the Atonement

Jonathan Edwards on the Atonement

Understanding the Legacy of America's Greatest Theologian

BRANDON JAMES CRAWFORD

Foreword by Joel Beeke

WIPF & STOCK · Eugene, Oregon

JONATHAN EDWARDS ON THE ATONEMENT
Understanding the Legacy of America's Greatest Theologian

Copyright © 2017 Brandon James Crawford. All rights reserved. Except for brief quotations in critical publications or reviews, no part of this book may be reproduced in any manner without prior written permission from the publisher. Write: Permissions, Wipf and Stock Publishers, 199 W. 8th Ave., Suite 3, Eugene, OR 97401.

Wipf & Stock
An Imprint of Wipf and Stock Publishers
199 W. 8th Ave., Suite 3
Eugene, OR 97401

www.wipfandstock.com

PAPERBACK ISBN: 978-1-5326-0997-8
HARDCOVER ISBN: 978-1-5326-0999-2
EBOOK ISBN: 978-1-5326-0998-5

Manufactured in the U.S.A.   FEBRUARY 9, 2017

Unless otherwise indicated, all Scripture quotations are from the The Holy Bible, King James Version (KJV).

Scripture quotations marked "ESV" are from the The Holy Bible, English Standard Version® (ESV®), copyright © 2001 by Crossway, a publishing ministry of Good News Publishers. All rights reserved. ESV Text Edition: 2011.

To Melanie

*She is far more precious than jewels.
The heart of her husband trusts in her,
and he will have no lack of gain.
She does him good, and not harm,
all the days of her life.*

(Proverbs 31:10–12 ESV)

Contents

Foreword by Joel Beeke | ix
Preface | xi

Introduction: A Legacy in Dispute | 1

PART 1: The Doctrine of Atonement Prior to Jonathan Edwards

Chapter 1 Early and Medieval Perspectives | 13
Chapter 2 Reformation and Puritan Perspectives | 34
Chapter 3 Alternative Perspectives in the Reformation and Puritan Eras | 53

PART 2: The Doctrine of Atonement in the Works of Jonathan Edwards

Chapter 4 The Basic Framework of Edwards's Doctrine of Atonement, Part 1—God | 73
Chapter 5 The Basic Framework of Edwards's Doctrine of Atonement, Part 2—Man, Sin, and Christ | 86
Chapter 6 The Vital Content of Edwards's Doctrine of Atonement | 106
Chapter 7 Additional Emphases in Edwards's Doctrine of Atonement | 129

Conclusion: What Is Jonathan Edwards's Legacy on the Atonement? | 137

Bibliography | 143

Foreword

JONATHAN EDWARDS TOWERS LIKE a giant over the field of American theology. His massive *Works* published by Yale (not to mention his many unpublished manuscripts) has proven to be the seedbed for an exponentially growing body of theological, missiological, philosophical, and historical literature produced by scholars from all over the world. The penetrating depth of Edwards's mind rivals that of the greatest thinkers of history. The vigor of his experiential spirituality burns like a brilliant lamp set on a stand. His articulation of Reformed doctrines according to the demands of evangelical revivals and Enlightenment criticisms continues to stimulate students of Reformed theology. Those who love the writings of the Puritans often find in Edwards a virtuoso of Puritan divinity, born out of time. Most significantly, Edwards was a giant in the field of biblical interpretation, constantly reflecting upon the Word of God in order to seek a systematic understanding of God insofar as he has revealed his ways.

Yet people have a tendency to sling stones at giants, and Edwards's theological legacy has not escaped such challenges. The divines who took up Edwards's mantle after his death, such as Samuel Hopkins and Joseph Bellamy, shifted away from the Reformed view of Christ's atonement as penal satisfaction and moved towards a governmental view more in line with the Arminian theology of Hugo Grotius. The former view holds that Christ, in order to satisfy God's justice on behalf of the elect, offered to God the obedience required by God's law and suffered the penalty threatened by that same law. The latter view holds that Christ's sinless sufferings made it possible for God to forgive sinners without dishonoring God's moral government of the world. While the satisfaction view includes elements of governmental concern (satisfying God's justice does glorify him as the righteous ruler), the governmental view denies that Christ satisfied the demands of God's law as the substitute of his people.

Scholars have detected some governmental language in Edwards's own writings on the atonement. This then raises questions. Did the "New Divinity" perspective on Christ's atonement arise from the theologian of Northampton? Was Edwards a champion of orthodoxy regarding Christ's sacrifice, or was he the vanguard of a Grotian invasion into Reformed theological territory? Or, perhaps we should ask, did Edwards's efforts to rationally defend Reformed doctrine actually undermine it on this crucial point of Christ's saving work?

Brandon Crawford has studied Edwards's doctrine of the atonement carefully, both in the context of its historical precedents and Edwards's broader theology. The fruit of Crawford's research is a helpful contribution to the debate over the roots of the New Divinity. Yet it is more. Just as John Owen's attempt to refute the universal view of Christ's redemption resulted in a rich exposition of Christ's sacrifice, so Brandon's examination of Edwards regarding the governmental theory has produced an exposition of his whole doctrine of the atonement.

Here then is a rich description of the teaching of one of our greatest divines regarding the most important locus of theological reflection: the meaning of Christ's cross. I gladly commend it to your reading.

Joel Beeke
President
Puritan Reformed Theological Seminary
Grand Rapids, Michigan

Preface

I WAS A FRESHMAN in college when the terrorists attacked on September 11, 2001. My friend John, who had graduated from high school with me just a few months earlier, joined the Marines and became part of the first wave of soldiers into Afghanistan. Though there were interruptions, he and I were able to keep in touch by email throughout his tour of duty. One day I received an email from John telling me about a sermon he had just listened to called "Doing Missions When Dying Is Gain," by a pastor named John Piper. I had never heard of John Piper before, but the sermon had made a tremendous impact on my friend's life, and he was insisting that I listen to it as well. I was able to track the sermon down, and heard it for myself. It was as transformative for me as it was for my friend. John Piper spoke of the glory of God, and the glory of the biblical mission, with a fervor that I had not heard before. After listening to that sermon, I knew I wanted to hear more from this man.

This led me to purchase my first book by John Piper, which was his classic work, *Desiring God*. While I wasn't sure I liked the term "Christian hedonism," my heart was resonating with the book's message. The endorsement on the back cover by J. I. Packer also peaked my interest. He wrote, "Jonathan Edwards, whose ghost walks through most of Piper's pages, would be delighted with his disciple." If John Piper's writings were finding their inspiration from Jonathan Edwards, I knew where my intellectual journey was headed next!

I started with a few biographies of Jonathan Edwards to learn more about the man. At the time, all I knew about Edwards was that he had a part in the Great Awakening and that he had preached a fiery sermon called

Preface

"Sinners in the Hands of an Angry God." Iain Murry's work *Jonathan Edwards: A New Biography* was the first I read. The book made an instant Edwards disciple out of me. Later, I picked up George Marsden's *Jonathan Edwards: A Life*, which expanded my understanding even more. As I continued learning more about Edwards from the secondary literature, I also began reading Edwards's own written works. I started with his *Dissertation Concerning the End for Which God Created the World*, and went on from there. Though I sometimes found Edwards difficult to follow, the parts that I did understand were reshaping my worldview. I discovered in Edwards a reliable mentor for my own theological and ministerial development.

As I transitioned from college to seminary, I found myself signing up for virtually every elective that would increase my exposure to Edwards and his writings. I took courses with names like "History of Christianity in America," "History of Revival in America," and "Theological Systems in American Church History." By the time I was ready for ThM studies, I knew that I wanted to make Edwards the focus of my research. The book that you now hold in your hands was born from the thesis I wrote for that ThM degree.

As I prepare to send this book out into the world, I want to offer a special thanks to all of those who have contributed to my knowledge of, and appreciation for, Jonathan Edwards. Thank you, Pastor Steven Thomas, for inspiring me all those years at Huron Baptist Church with your "Edwardsesque" preaching and teaching ministry. Thank you, John Piper, for "making my heart sing" (to use one of your phrases) with your Edwards-inspired writings. Thank you, Gerald Priest, for offering all those church history electives in seminary! Thank you Joel Beeke, Michael Haykin, Adriaan Neele, and Dolf Britz, all Edwards enthusiasts who taught me, motivated me, and challenged me during my ThM studies. Thank you, Jonathan Edwards, for committing so many of your remarkable thoughts to paper. Thank you for teaching me how to be a biblically rooted pastor-theologian. And finally, a very special thanks to my wife, Melanie, for encouraging me to pursue my passion even when it required great sacrifice on her part. *Soli Deo Gloria*.

Brandon James Crawford
November 1, 2016

Introduction
A Legacy in Dispute

JONATHAN EDWARDS, "AMERICA'S MOST penetrating, rigorous, and subtle theologian,"[1] completed his earthly course on March 22, 1758. After he died, his wife Sarah penned a brief note to their daughter Esther sharing the news. Sarah wrote, "O my very dear child, What shall I say? A holy and good God has covered us with a dark cloud.... The Lord has done it. He has made me adore his goodness, that we had him so long. But my God lives; and he has my heart." Then she offered these final, memorable words: "Oh what a legacy my husband, and your father, has left us!"[2]

THE RISE OF THE EDWARDEANS

Edwards did indeed leave a remarkable legacy. Before his death he pastored three churches, raised a large family, led a Great Awakening, mentored aspiring ministers, presided over a college, and produced a vast treasury of theological literature that continues to be studied to this day. Unfortunately, he did *not* leave any clear intellectual successors behind.[3] What he left instead was a band of brothers now called the "Edwardeans."

---

1. Schwartz, "New and Noteworthy," 91–92.
2. Quoted in Marsden, *Jonathan Edwards*, 495.
3. This assertion was made by Mark Noll in *The Scandal of the Evangelical Mind*, 24, and represents the consensus opinion among Edwards scholars.

Introduction

The first of these was a brilliant but "unpolished" young man named Joseph Bellamy (1719–1790), who hailed from Cheshire, Connecticut. After graduating from Yale in 1735, he moved into the Edwards home to complete his ministerial training as Jonathan's apprentice, which was a common practice in that day.[4] Though he was only a part of the Edwards household for a brief time, Jonathan Edwards had a lasting influence on him and the two remained close friends for the rest of Edwards's life. Like his mentor, Bellamy became an author as well as a pastor. After completing a book entitled *True Religion Delineated* in 1750, Bellamy sent the manuscript over to Edwards for review. The book had a similar aim to Edwards's *Religious Affections*, published four years earlier, in that both works sought to provide a framework for distinguishing genuine Christianity from its counterfeits—though Bellamy's method of argumentation differed from Edwards's.[5] Edwards reviewed the work of his former apprentice as requested and contributed a glowing preface.

Another of Edwards's young protégés was a man named Samuel Hopkins (1721–1803) of Waterbury, Connecticut. Hopkins was deeply moved by the commencement address Edwards delivered to his graduating class at Yale, and so he, too, decided to complete his ministerial preparation under Edwards's guidance. He arrived at the Edwards home in December of 1741, and remained there for a number of months. After a brief period as an itinerant preacher he was installed as the pastor of the church in Housatonic, Massachusetts, just seven miles from Northampton, which allowed him to return to the Edwards home frequently for dinner and conversation with Edwards and his family.[6]

It has been said that Hopkins "was probably the least celebrated, and least talented [of the Edwardeans] . . . as a preacher, but he more than

---

4. Edwards wrote of Joseph Bellamy in 1754, "Mr. Bellamy is in some respects a little unpolished; yet he is a man of such gifts and grace, such activity, resolution, attended with sagacity and prudence, that I know of no man in any measure so likely to be a means of uniting that congregation [a Presbyterian congregation in New York], and maintaining its peace, of greatly increasing it and very much promoting the interest of religion in that flourishing town as he." *Letters* no. 184, in *Works*, 16:619. The Reverend Ezra Stiles was less gracious: "He was of a haughty domineering temper and till of late years uncensorious of his brethren in the ministry and others who opposed him . . . of a dogmatical and overbearing disposition." In Dexter, ed., *Literary Diary of Ezra Stiles*, 3:384–85.

5. The work was originally published in Boston, Massachusetts, by the Congregational Board of Publication.

6. Dodd, *Marriage to a Difficult Man*, 165.

INTRODUCTION

made up for that in theological acumen."[7] Like Bellamy and his mentor, he too became an accomplished author. In fact, he became Jonathan Edwards's first biographer, providing the only substantive firsthand accounts of the Edwards household available today. He remembered Edwards as a man with "an uncommon thirst for knowledge; in the pursuit of which he spared no cost or pains"; a man who "read all the books, especially books of divinity, that he could come at, from which he could hope to get any help in his pursuit of knowledge." "But," Hopkins said, "he studied the Bible more than all other books, and more than most other divines do." He noted that Edwards was an original thinker, a prolific writer, and a reserved, yet thoughtful, conversationalist; an attentive father, a devoted husband, and a good neighbor. His biography also offers us insights into Edwards's intellectual outlook. He remembered Edwards as "a rigid Calvinist" who "judged that nothing was wanting, but to have these doctrines properly stated, and judiciously and well defined, in order to their appearing most agreeable to reason and common sense, as well as the doctrines of revelation; and that this therefore was the only effectual method to convince, or silence and shame the opposers of them."[8]

Coming of age just a few years after Bellamy and Hopkins were two more apprentices: Jonathan Edwards Jr. and Timothy Dwight. The former was the second son of Jonathan Edwards. He was born in Northampton, Massachusetts, in 1745, but was raised by his family in the town of Stockbridge. From the pages of Hopkins's biography we gain a sense of the early training Jonathan the Younger received from his father. Hopkins wrote that Edwards would start each morning by gathering his entire family together for a time of prayer and Scripture reading, "upon which he asked his children questions according to their age and capacity; and took occasion to explain some passages . . . or enforce any duty recommended, &c. as he thought most proper." On other occasions,

> He took opportunities to treat with them in his study, singly and particularly, about their own soul's concerns; and to give them warning, exhortation, and direction, as he saw occasion. He took

---

7. Sweeney and Guelzo, eds., *New England Theology*, 86.

8. Hopkins, *Life and Character*, 43–44; 57–58. Edwards's study habits seem to have rubbed off on his protégés. In 1745, Bellamy wrote that "the delusions which I saw take place in New Light times have engaged me, as well [as] the divided state of the Christian world in general, to devote my whole time for above twenty years to enquire into the nature of Christianity. I have conversed with all men of genius" and "have read all the books I could come at." Quoted in Valeri, *Law and Providence in Joseph Bellamy's New England*, 48.

much pain to instruct them in the principles of religion; in which he made use of the *Assembly's Shorter Catechism*: not merely by taking care that they learned it by heart, but by leading them into an understanding of the doctrines therein taught, by asking them questions on each answer, and explaining it to them.[9]

In April of 1755, Edwards sent his son on a missionary expedition with his friend Gideon Hawley, probably in the hopes of stirring missionary interest in his child. About a month into that trip Edwards sent a very tender letter to Jonathan Jr., expressing how much he missed him and offering a few words of instruction. The letter further illustrates the kind of mentorship that Jonathan Jr. received in his early years. His father wrote,

> Always set God before your eyes, and live in his fear, and seek him every day with all diligence: for 'tis he, and he only can make you happy or miserable, as he pleases; and your life and health, and the eternal salvation of your soul, and your all in this life and that which is to come, depends on his will and pleasure. . . . Remember what Christ has said, that you must be born again, or you never can see the kingdom of God. Never give yourself any rest, unless you have good evidence that you are converted and become a new creature. We hope that God will preserve your life and health, and return you to Stockbridge again in safety; but always remember that life is uncertain: you know not how soon you must die, and therefore had need to be always ready.[10]

Jonathan Jr. lost his father when he was just thirteen years old, but his theological instruction did not come to an end. In 1765 he matriculated at Princeton College (becoming the only direct disciple of Edwards not to attend Yale) and thereafter took an apprenticeship under Joseph Bellamy. After many years in the pastorate, Jonathan the Younger went on to become the president of Union College in New York, passing away three years later, in 1801.

Timothy Dwight (1752–1817), the "genial giant,"[11] was born in Northampton, Massachusetts, to Edwards's daughter Mary. Though Timothy was too young to be mentored by Edwards the way Joseph Bellamy, Samuel Hopkins, and Jonathan Jr. had been, his mother raised him "to champion her father's clerical concerns." And, as he grew up, she "made

---

9. Hopkins, *Life and Character*, 46–47.
10. Edwards, *Letters* no. 204, in *Works of Jonathan Edwards*, 6:666–67.
11. Dodd, *Marriage to a Difficult Man*, 149.

INTRODUCTION

sure he would follow in his grandfather's footsteps by sending him to Yale and encouraging his tutelage with her brother [and Edwards's son] Jonathan Jr."[12] Dwight eventually became the president of Yale, witnessing the conversion of hundreds of students during his tenure there, and he saw his chapel sermons published as a five-volume set entitled *Theology Explained and Defended*—a set that remained very popular in evangelical academic circles for a number of years.[13]

Through the influence of Bellamy and Hopkins, many more Edwardeans would emerge. John Smalley (1734–1820), first introduced to the theology of Edwards by his minister, Eleazar Wheelock, headed for Yale in 1752, and thereafter took an apprenticeship under Bellamy. He enjoyed a long and fruitful ministry, culminating in the publication of his sermons in a popular multivolume set.[14] Nathan Strong (1748–1816) was also mentored by Bellamy and went on to serve the First Church of Hartford, Connecticut. In addition to his pastoral work, he organized the Connecticut Missionary Society, launched a missions magazine, and published his sermons in a two-volume set.

Another man, Nathaniel Emmons (1745–1840), headed to Yale in 1763, where he fell under the spell of Edwards's treatise *Freedom of the Will*. After graduation, he took an apprenticeship first under Nathan Strong, and then under John Smalley, two Edwardeans "who made Emmons 'a thorough convert to [Edwards's] scheme of sentiments.'"[15] Stephen West (1735–1819) graduated from Yale in 1755, and under the tutelage of Samuel Hopkins became "as thoroughgoing a convert to Edwardseanism as Hopkins," and in due course published his famous work, *Scripture Doctrine of the Atonement, Proposed to Careful Examination*.[16] Nathaniel Taylor (1786–1858) entered Yale in 1800, was converted some years later under the ministry of Timothy Dwight, lived with Dwight for two years, and "[d]uring the next ten years ... became one of the leading Congregationalists in New England."[17]

---

12. Sweeney and Guelzo, *New England Theology*, 189.

13. A modern reprint edition is presently available. See Dwight, *Theology Explained and Defended*, 5 vols (London: Forgotten Books, 2012).

14. Sweeney and Guelzo, *New England Theology*, 144.

15. Ibid., 113.

16. The book is still available in a reprint edition through Forgotten Books.

17. Sweeney and Guelzo, *New England Theology*, 195.

INTRODUCTION

And then there was Edwards Amasa Park (1808–1900), the "last Edwardsian,"[18] who married one of Edwards's great-granddaughters, studied theology under Nathaniel Taylor, and became a professor at Andover Seminary in Massachusetts. Park immersed himself in the study of Edwards and his successors, publishing a number of volumes on the subject, the most acclaimed of which was his work entitled *The Atonement: Discourses and Treatises*.[19]

Together, through their pulpits, professorships, and publications, these Edwardians, also known as the "New Divinity" men or "consistent Calvinists," would dominate the theological conversation in New England for nearly a hundred years.[20] Though not exactly like their mentor, their ministries did parallel his in many ways; and like him, they made it their aim to vindicate evangelical Calvinism over and against the rising tide of Arminianism, Liberalism, and "enthusiasm" by securing the Reformed faith to a "reasonable" foundation, which, it was believed, would more successfully commend the Reformed faith to their "enlightened" age.

THE EDWARDEANS ON THE ATONEMENT

Reconciling the Calvinistic conception of divine sovereignty with modern conceptions of human autonomy, without surrendering either one, was a particular concern for the Edwardeans.[21] They were quite sensitive to the charges of "inequity" and "injustice" which befell the Old Calvinist system, and were determined to craft a new system that would be more "reasonable" to enlightened men. They sensed a particularly compelling need to reframe the doctrine of atonement along more "scientific" or "consistent" lines, seeing that the Old Calvinist notion of a definite, penal substitutionary atonement was particularly offensive to modern thinkers.

The Edwardeans' solution was to abandon classic Reformed teaching on the atonement in favor of a modified "governmental" theory. Originally

---

18. Crisp and Sweeney, eds., *After Jonathan Edwards*, 151.

19. Park's work was published by the Congregational Publishing Society in 1859.

20. Indeed, Sweeney and Guelzo argue that "The New England Theology remains the most significant and enduring Christian theological school of thought to have originated in the United States." *New England Theology*, 4. For a more thorough listing of the New Divinity's leading lights, see Conforti, *Samuel Hopkins and the New Divinity Movement*, 227–32.

21. Samuel Hopkins's first treatise was on this very subject, published as *A Bold Push: In a Letter to the Author of a Late Pamphlet, Intitled, Fair Play*, in 1758.

proposed by the sixteenth-century theologian Hugo Grotius, the governmental theory suggests that Christ, through his death, served as a penal *example* rather than a penal *substitute*. He died to demonstrate "God's aversion to sin," paying respect to God's law and at the same time providing men with an inducement to repent. In this theory, sin is not a crime against God himself, but an act against "the divine government,"[22] and Christ's work does not *secure* the salvation of *anyone*, but makes salvation *possible* for *everyone*, without negating the sovereignty of God in salvation. In his work *The Atonement*, Edwards Amasa Park further explained the theory with these nine propositions:

> First, our Lord suffered pains which were substituted for the penalty of the law, and may be called punishment in the more general sense of that word, but were not, strictly and literally, the penalty which the law had threatened.
>
> Secondly, the sufferings of our Lord satisfied the general justice of God, but did not satisfy his distributive justice.
>
> Thirdly, the humiliation, pains, and death of our Redeemer were equivalent in meaning to the punishment threatened in the moral law, and thus they satisfied Him who is determined to maintain the honor of this law, but they did not satisfy the demands of the law itself for our punishment.
>
> Fourthly, the active obedience, viewed as the holiness, of Christ was honorable to the law, but was not a work of supererogation, performed by our Substitute, and then transferred and imputed to us, so as to satisfy the requisitions of the law for our own active obedience...
>
> Fifthly, the law and the distributive justice of God, although honored by the life and death of Christ, will yet eternally demand the punishment of every one who has sinned.
>
> Sixthly, the atonement rendered it consistent and desirable for God to save all who exercise evangelical faith, yet it did not render it obligatory on Him, in distributive justice to save them.
>
> Seventhly, the atonement was designed for the welfare of all men; to make the eternal salvation of all men possible; to remove all the obstacles which the honor of the law and of distributive justice presented against the salvation of the non-elect as well as the elect.
>
> Eighthly, the atonement does not constitute the reason why some men are regenerated, and others not, but this reason is found only in the sovereign, electing will of God...
>
> Ninthly, the atonement is *useful* on men's account, and in order to furnish new motives to holiness, but it is *necessary* on

---

22. Breitenback, "Consistent Calvinism of the New Divinity Movement," 249.

God's account, and in order to *enable* him, as a consistent Ruler, to pardon any, even the smallest sin, and therefore to bestow on sinners any, even the smallest favor.²³

THE PERENNIAL QUESTION

The perennial question, of course, concerns the extent to which Edwards influenced the Edwardeans to embrace these principles. We know that Edwards had no true intellectual successors. But did the trajectory of his thinking head in the direction of the governmental theory, or did the Edwardeans significantly depart from the trajectory he set? Why did none of them embrace classic Reformed orthodoxy?

Edwards Amasa Park believed that "certain germs of [the Edwardean doctrine of atonement] are found in the writings of the elder Edwards," but not the whole system. The Edwardean system, he argued, was more "harmonious with itself," "more precise, unequivocal, scientific" than was Edwards's doctrinal formulation.²⁴

Of course, not all have shared Park's view. Several decades after Park penned his words, the famous Princeton scholar B. B. Warfield took just the opposite view. He believed that the Edwardeans actually *forsook* Edwards's teaching, "becoming the earnest advocate[s] of . . . opinions which [Edwards] gained his chief celebrity in demolishing." Warfield was adamant that Edwards was not responsible for the popularization of the governmental theory, and should in no way be associated with it. The Edwardean doctrine of atonement was a "perversion" of Edwards's doctrine, Warfield said.²⁵

Dorus Paul Rudisill, whose 1971 work entitled *The Doctrine of Atonement in Jonathan Edwards and His Successors* remains the only book-length treatment of the question, reached a more nuanced conclusion. He notes "Edwards did not attack any view presented by a then living theologian nor was he attacked by any contemporary New England Calvinist for his view," indicating that "the divergence of Edwards' doctrine from the orthodox view of New England was not marked enough to demand a rebuttal, if a divergence were noticed at all."²⁶ Even so, he does conclude that Edwards made at least a small contribution to the Edwardean view, contending that

---

23. Park, *Atonement*, x–xi.

24. Ibid., ix. Park makes no attempt to hide his own theological bias in his assessment.

25. Warfield, *Studies in Theology*, 532–36. The work is a collection of previously published articles made available in a new, single volume.

26. Rudisill, *Doctrine of the Atonement*, 21.

"the Edwardeans find support in President Edwards for those elements which constitute the framework of the theory [which include his views on 'the nature of law, love as the all-controlling attribute of God, Christ's passion as the whole substance of the Atonement, and sovereignty in applying the Atonement']," while finding no support at all "with respect to those elements which form the vital substance of an Atonement theory [i.e., the questions of the necessity, nature, and extent of the atonement]."[27]

John Gerstner, writing in 1987, also held a nuanced view, though his view does seem to favor Warfield's conclusion over that of Park's or Rudisill's. Gerstner writes that the Edwardeans "championed the governmental (Grotian) theory of the atonement, thinking they had Jonathan Edwards as father . . . yet without justification." In his opinion, while elements of Edwards's writings may have included some echoes of Grotius, when the larger context of Edwards's theological system is brought to bear upon the subject it becomes clear that Edwards's doctrine bears little similarity to that of his successors.[28]

More recently, Oliver Crisp has offered his perspective on the relationship between Edwards and the Edwardeans, arguing that there are indeed clear lines of continuity between the two, to the point that Edwards both knew and approved of the ideas put forward by the Edwardeans:

> The seeds of the New England governmental view of the atonement were sown by Edwards himself. But he did not have the opportunity, or perhaps the inclination, to develop this in his own work. So the views expressed by Bellamy, Samuel Hopkins, and Jonathan Edwards Jr . . . were, one might think, a doctrinal innovation in one respect. But they were building on some ideas latent in the work of Edwards Senior, and they did, it appears, have his sanction for doing so. Here, then, is an instance of theological development that, though complex, does not bespeak some sort of declension, or departure from the teaching of the master.[29]

THE AIM OF THIS STUDY

Many factors have contributed to the ongoing lack of consensus on this question. Ironically, one of the *leading* factors is our continued ignorance of

---

27. Ibid., 125–27.
28. Gerstner, *Jonathan Edwards*, 59–60.
29. Crisp, "Moral Government of God," 78–79.

Introduction

Edwards's true theological perspective, due in large measure to the paucity of literature examining his doctrine of atonement on its own terms. Mark Hamilton makes this point in a recent article. There is a "perennial fascination" with "the doctrinal formulations of Anselm, Abelard, Thomas and Calvin," he writes, while "signally absent from this list is the name Jonathan Edwards." How could this be? "Until recently," he writes, "Edwards' doctrine of atonement has been primarily a matter of historical interest, propelled mainly by questions of his doctrinal relationship to his intellectual progeny in the New England theology. Such decidedly historical interest has resulted in a tendency to interpret Edwards' doctrine of atonement in light of his successors. For this reason . . . Edwards' contribution remains largely overlooked."[30]

The present study aims to address this problem by offering a thorough presentation of Edwards's doctrine of atonement as revealed in his collected works. The first three chapters will set the historical context for Edwards's doctrine by surveying the teachings of his predecessors. In the chapters that follow, Edwards's own writings will be explored. Chapters 4 and 5 will survey the "basic framework" of his doctrine, chapter 6 will explore its "vital content," and chapter 7 will consider some "additional emphases" of his doctrine. A concluding section will recapitulate Edwards's contributions and offer a few summary thoughts.

The potential benefits of this study should be apparent. First, this study should begin to fill that significant lacuna in our understanding of Edwards's doctrinal perspective. If it also serves to generate interest in this subject from other authors, the profit will be greater still. Additionally, if Edwards's doctrine of atonement can be established with a reasonable degree of certainty, we should also find it easier to answer the historical question surrounding Edwards and the Edwardeans. Fourthly, it is hoped that this study will spawn greater interest in the doctrine of atonement in general. The atonement is the heart of the gospel, and the gospel is the heart of the Christian faith. No doctrine is more worthy of our reflection, affection, and careful application than this one.

---

30. Hamilton, "Jonathan Edwards on the Atonement," 394. Reference was made earlier to Rudisill's book-length treatment of this question. Remarkably, even in that book, the section detailing Edwards's doctrine of atonement is only twenty-three pages in length, with a three-page "recapitulation" at the end of the book.

Part 1

The Doctrine of Atonement Prior to Jonathan Edwards

PART 1

Chapter 1

Early and Medieval Perspectives

SPEAKING AT TYNDALE HOUSE in 1973, J. I. Packer noted that "every theological question has behind it a history of study."[1] This is particularly true of the doctrine of Christ's atonement. Since the days of the apostles, Christ's followers have been pondering the significance of his death, trying to apprehend precisely what that death accomplished and how its spiritual blessings are received. Wise men study this history and gain important insights from it. Sometimes, however, the work can be difficult.

Coming to terms with the *early* church's understanding of the atonement can be particularly daunting, because so little was written on the subject during that era. In fact, all we really have from the church's early centuries is a handful of passages scattered about in various letters and treatises, along with a statement or two in the early creeds—but even these do not delve into specifics. Historian Jaroslav Pelikan illustrates the challenge: "The creed adopted at Nicea [in A.D. 325] confessed that it had been 'for the sake of us men and for the purpose of our salvation' that Christ 'came down [from heaven]'. . . . But neither it nor later dogmas specified in any detail just how the salvation which was the purpose of Christ's coming was related to these events in his

---

1. This lecture was subsequently published as an article: "What Did the Cross Achieve?: The Logic of Penal Substitution," *TB* 25 (1974) 3–45. The reader should note that the present chapter is intended only as a brief survey of the early and medieval church's teachings on the doctrine of atonement in order to set the stage for Jonathan Edwards's contributions to the doctrine. Additional general surveys of this topic can be found in Berkhof, *History of Christian Doctrines*, 165–99; Allison, "History of the Doctrine of the Atonement," 4–19; and Jeffery, Ovey, and Sach, *Pierced for Our Transgressions*, 161–203. A more thorough treatment of the subject is available in Grensted's work *A Short History of the Doctrine of the Atonement*.

earthly and heavenly states." As a result, the doctrine of Christ's atonement remained, to a large extent, "dogmatically undefined."[2]

This does not mean that the doctrine of atonement was unimportant to the early church, of course. One of the early church fathers, Tertullian, even went so far as to say that Christ's atonement is the heart of the Christian faith.[3] Early leaders simply did not have the time or opportunity for extended reflection on this doctrine, given the Trinitarian controversies of the day. What follows is a brief survey of those early Christian references to the doctrine, followed by the more substantive treatments from the church's medieval era.

THE ANTE-NICENE FATHERS

The age of the Ante-Nicene Fathers stretches from the close of the apostolic age to the adoption of the Nicene Creed in A.D. 325. Though no sustained treatments of the atonement are to be found during this period, several scattered references in the various letters and treatises of these church fathers are worthy of note.

Clement of Rome (d. A.D. 99)

Clement of Rome enjoys pride of place among the early church fathers.[4] His *First Epistle to the Corinthians*, written around A.D. 95–97, is generally considered the oldest extant Christian writing outside of the New Testament. Though not a doctrinal epistle, it does contain several important references to Christ's atonement. In the twenty-first chapter of the letter, after quoting the messianic prophecy of Isaiah 53, for example, Clement writes, "Let us reverence the Lord Jesus Christ, whose blood was given for us."[5] And a little later in the epistle, he adds this: "In love has the Lord taken us to Himself. On account of the Love he bore us, Jesus Christ our Lord gave

---

2. Pelikan, *Emergence of the Catholic Tradition*, 141.

3. Tertullian, *Against Marcion* 3.8, in *Ante-Nicene Fathers*, 3:328. Tertullian's perspective on the atonement will be discussed in brief later in the chapter.

4. Eusebius believed Clement of Rome to be the associate of Paul mentioned in Phil 4:3. See his *Ecclesiastical History* 3.15. Historian J. B. Lightfoot rejects this suggestion on geographical, chronological, and historical grounds in his *Saint Paul's Epistle to the Philippians*, 168–69.

5. Clement, *Epistle to the Corinthians* 21, in *Ante-Nicene Fathers*, 1:11.

his blood for us by the will of God; His flesh for our flesh, and His soul for our souls."[6] While there is certainly some ambiguity here, his statements do still indicate a fairly developed understanding of Christ's atoning work. He understood Christ's death as a loving sacrifice, foretold by prophecy, implemented by the will of God, and involving an act of substitution. Christ gave "his flesh for our flesh, his soul for our souls."[7]

The Epistle of Barnabas (ca. A.D. 100)

Though purporting to come from the biblical Barnabas, internal evidence suggests that this epistle came from another man's pen.[8] Its contents are preoccupied with demonstrating the obsolescence of the Mosaic system, as well as proving that Christ and his New Testament church are the fulfillment of all Old Testament types and prophecies. Mingled with these themes, however, are a few significant references to Christ's death. In one place, the author writes, "If therefore the Son of God, who is Lord, and who will judge the living and the dead, suffered, that His stroke might give us life, let us believe that the Son of God could not have suffered except for our sakes." And a few sentences later, he adds this: "He also Himself was to offer in sacrifice for our sins the vessel of the Spirit, in order that the type established in Isaac when he was offered upon the altar might be fully accomplished."[9]

---

6. Ibid., 49, in *Ante-Nicene Fathers*, 1:18.

7. Grensted argues that Clement held to a "moral theory" of the atonement, which teaches that Christ's death was about displaying the love of God for sinners, persuading them to respond in repentance and faith. He quotes passages like the following from the seventh chapter of Clement's letter: "Let us fix our eyes on the blood of Christ and understand how precious it is unto His Father, because being shed for our salvation it won for the whole world the grace of repentance." *Short History of the Doctrine of Atonement*, 12. It appears, however, that Grensted is conflating Clement's understanding of the *meaning* of the cross with the moral exhortations he offers *in light of* the cross. His doctrine of the cross was substitutionary. His exhortation was to appreciate how "precious" the cross is because of that fact. Nowhere do the early church fathers present the cross as a mere demonstration of divine love. Instead, they present the cross as having objectively *accomplished* something. This error seems to be repeated in his interactions with other church fathers.

8. The internal evidence includes "the numerous inaccuracies which it contains with respect to Mosaic enactments and observances—the absurd and trifling interpretations of Scripture which it suggests—and the many silly vaunts of superior knowledge in which its writer indulges." "Introductory Note to the Epistle of Barnabas," in *Ante-Nicene Fathers*, 1:134.

9. *Epistle of Barnabas* 7, in *Ante-Nicene Fathers*, 1:141.

At least two points are worthy of note here. First, the author understood Christ's death as a sacrificial offering for human sin. As he explained, Christ died "for our sakes" and "in sacrifice for our sins." Additionally, his words indicate that he believed Christ's death was a sacrifice for *actual* sins, not just for sin in general, and that *Christ's* death successfully removed the penalty of death for *other* human beings. This is evident in his statement that Christ's death "gives us life." In short, he too understood Christ's atonement in substitutionary terms.

Ignatius (d. ca. A.D. 107)

Ignatius of Antioch, a disciple of the apostle John, wrote a series of church epistles on his way to Rome, where he would face martyrdom. One of these letters, his *Epistle to the Smyrnaeans*, contains a statement about Christ's death that, while vague, indicates that he also understood the event as a substitutionary act that secured the salvation of men. He writes, "Now, He suffered all these things for our sakes, that we might be saved. And He suffered truly, even as also He truly raised up Himself, not, as certain unbelievers maintain, that He only seemed to suffer, as they themselves only seem to be [Christians]."[10]

In another of his letters, his *Epistle to the Trallians*, we find this statement about Christ's death, with its clear allusions to 2 Timothy 2:6 and 1 John 1:9: "Become imitators of his sufferings, and of His love, wherewith He loved us when He gave Himself a ransom for us, that He might cleanse us by His blood from our old ungodliness, and bestow life on us when we were almost on the point of perishing through the depravity that was in us."[11] Here we have clear descriptions of Christ's death as a voluntary act, a loving act, and a "ransom" that saved others from death—though he does not specify the precise nature of the ransom or to whom the ransom was paid.

Epistle to Diognetus (ca. A.D. 130)

The authorship of the *Epistle to Diognetus* is unknown, the writer identifying himself only as "Mathetes."[12] The letter is largely an apologetical work

---

10. Ignatius, *Epistle to the Smyrnaeans* 9, in *Ante-Nicene Fathers*, 1:87.
11. Ignatius, *Letter to the Trallians* 8, in *Ante-Nicene Fathers*, 1:69.
12. "Mathetes" is the Greek word for "disciple."

that makes a case for the superiority of Christianity over its predecessor, Judaism. The epistle also explains the customs of Christians and commends the Christian faith to the non-Christian world. In the ninth chapter of the work, we also find a striking passage on the atonement:

> When our wickedness had reached its height, and it had been clearly shown that its reward, punishment and death, was impending over us; and when the time had come which God had before appointed for manifesting His own kindness and power, how the one love of God, through exceeding regard for men, did not regard us with hatred, nor thrust us away, nor remember our iniquity against us, but showed great long-suffering, and bore with us, He Himself took on Him the burden of our iniquities, He gave His own Son as a ransom for us, the holy One for transgressors, the blameless One for the wicked, the righteous One for the unrighteous, the incorruptible One for the corruptible, the immortal One for them that are mortal. For what other thing was capable of covering our sins than His righteousness? By what other one was it possible that we, the wicked and ungodly, could be justified, than by the only Son of God? O sweet exchange! O unsearchable operation! O benefits surpassing all expectation! That the wickedness of many should be hid in a single righteous One, and that the righteousness of One should justify many transgressors![13]

Though Christ's death is not explicitly mentioned in this passage, it is clearly implied by the context. The affirmations that he makes about Christ's death are also quite clear. Christ is the "Son of God" who was sent by his Father in love to provide the solution for "our wickedness" and the "punishment and death" that our wickedness visits upon us. That solution, the author says, was to make a "sweet exchange": The "punishment and death" owing to humans "He Himself took on Him," the Son serving as a "ransom" for sin, "covering" sins over so that "the wicked and ungodly could be justified." In this exchange the "blameless," "righteous," "incorruptible" one took our punishment and gave us his righteousness in its place. Commenting on these remarkable statements, historian John Aloisi writes, "*The Epistle to Diognetus* provides a clear example of belief in penal substitution at a very early point in church history."[14]

---

13. *Epistle to Diognetus* 9, in *Ante-Nicene Fathers*, 1:28.
14. Aloisi, "His Flesh for Our Flesh," 40.

Polycarp (d. A.D. 155)

Polycarp, another disciple of the apostle John, wrote his *Epistle to the Philippians* in the early years of the second century, perhaps A.D. 115.[15] Several statements in this epistle provide glimpses into his understanding of Christ's death. For example, as his letter begins he writes, "I have greatly rejoiced with you in our Lord Jesus Christ . . . who for our sins suffered even unto death, [but] 'whom God raised from the dead, having loosed the bands of the grave.'"[16] And in another place he writes, "Let us then continually persevere in our hope, and the earnest of our righteousness, which is Jesus Christ, 'who bore our sins in His own body on the tree,' 'who did no sin, neither was there guile found in His mouth,' but endured all things for us, that we might live in Him."[17] Then, in the ninth chapter of the epistle, he challenges his readers to follow the example of the martyrs, who "loved not this present world, but Him who died for us, and for our sakes was raised again by God from the dead."[18] Like many other church fathers, Polycarp uses the language of Scripture to explain the meaning of Christ's death. These, supplemented with his own clarifying comments, seem to suggest that he, too, embraced a substitutionary understanding of the atonement. Christ is the sinless one who "bore our sins in his own body," who died so that others could live.

Justin Martyr (d. A.D. 165)

Justin Martyr's *Dialogue with Trypho* was "the first elaborate exposition of the reasons for regarding Christ as the Messiah of the Old Testament, and the first systematic attempt to exhibit the false position of the Jews in regard to Christianity."[19] In the eighty-ninth chapter of this work, Justin focuses his attention on the offense of the cross. His Jewish conversation partner, Trypho, accepts the idea that the promised Messiah would have to suffer, but finds it difficult to accept the notion that the Messiah could be hanged from a tree—a fate that would mean he was accursed by God, according to

---

15. Hartog, *Polycarp and the New Testament*, 169.
16. Polycarp, *Epistle to the Philippians* 1, in *Ante-Nicene Fathers*, 1:33.
17. Ibid., 8, in *Ante-Nicene Fathers*, 1:35.
18. Ibid., 9, in *Ante-Nicene Fathers*, 1:35.
19. Roberts and Donaldson, "Introductory Note to the First Apology of Justin Martyr," in *Ante-Nicene Fathers*, 1:160.

the Scriptures. How could God's Messiah be accursed?[20] Justin responds that Jesus, the Messiah, became a curse not on account of his own sins, but "on account of the sins of the people," as it says in Isaiah 53.[21] As Trypho continues to express skepticism, Justin explains further:

> Just as God commanded the sign to be made by the brazen serpent, and yet He is blameless; even so, though a curse lies in the law against persons who are crucified, yet no curse lies on the Christ of God, by whom all that have committed things worthy of a curse are saved. For the whole human race will be found to be under a curse. For it is written in the law of Moses, 'Cursed is every one that continueth not in all things that are written in the book of the law to do them.' . . . If, then, the father of all wished His Christ for the whole human family to take upon Him the curses of all, knowing that, after He had been crucified and was dead, He would raise Him up, why do you argue about Him, who submitted to suffer these things according to the Father's will, as if He were accursed, and do not rather bewail yourselves?

This passage appears to represent an advance in the early church's understanding of the atonement. As Aloisi writes, "while Clement, Barnabas, and Polycarp provide examples of early believers who viewed Christ's death as a substitution for sinners, Justin is likely the first second-century writer to explicitly affirm that Christ bore the divine punishment for human sins upon the cross."[22] Thus, we can say that Justin Martyr was an early proponent of the penal substitution view of the atonement.

Irenaeus (d. A.D. 202)

Ever since Gustaf Aulen's lecture on Irenaeus's doctrine of atonement in 1930, the common view has been that Irenaeus was an early proponent of the so-called *Christus Victor* model of the atonement, which sees Christ's death not as a substitutionary sacrifice for sinners, but as part of a divine drama in which "Christ—Christus Victor—fights against and triumphs

---

20. Deut 21:23 says, "His body shall not remain all night upon the tree, but thou shalt in any wise bury him that day; (for he that is hanged *is* accursed of God)."
21. Justin Martyr, *Dialogue with Trypho* 89, in *Ante-Nicene Fathers*, 1:244.
22. Aloisi, "His Flesh for Our Flesh," 37.

PART 1: ATONEMENT PRIOR TO JONATHAN EDWARDS

over the evil powers of the world, the 'tyrants' under which mankind is in bondage and suffering, and in Him God reconciles the world to himself."[23]

Looking at the works of Irenaeus, we find that these themes are indeed present in his discussions about Christ. In his *Against Heresies*, for example, Irenaeus writes that Christ has "summed up all things, both waging war against our enemy, and crushing him who had at the beginning led us away captives in Adam, and trampled upon his head."[24] And again a few paragraphs later, "the apostate angel of God is destroyed by its [i.e., the Word of God's] voice, being exposed in his true colours, and vanquished by the Son of man keeping the commandment of God. For as in the beginning he enticed man to transgress his Maker's law, and thereby got him into his power," yet "he should, when conquered, be bound with the same chains with which he had bound man, in order that man, being set free, might return to his Lord . . . for when Satan is bound, man is free."[25] Irenaeus also describes the work of redemption as the story of man, "a vessel in his (Satan's) possession" and held "under his power," finally being "loosed from the bonds of condemnation" by the work of Christ.[26]

And yet, it would be a disservice to Irenaeus to suggest that the *Christus Victor* theme running through his teachings represents the beginning and end of his doctrine of atonement, for "much more central to his theology is the idea that Christ recapitulates humanity and thereby reverses the effects of Adam's sin."[27] This doctrine of "recapitulation," which was perhaps Irenaeus's most significant contribution to theology,[28] teaches that "by his incarnation and human life [Christ] . . . reverses the course on which Adam by his sin started humanity and thus becomes a new leaven in the life of mankind. He communicates immortality to those who are united to him

---

23. Aulen, *Christus Victor*, 6. Indeed, Aulen attempts to make the case that this "classic" conception of the atonement was the dominant view of the church for the first thousand years of its history. Others dispute this interpretation, however, including Aloisi, "His Flesh for our Flesh," 40–44; and Allison, "History of the Doctrine of the Atonement," 4–19.

24. Irenaeus, *Against Heresies* 5.21.1, in *Ante-Nicene Fathers*, 1:548.

25. Ibid., 5.21.3, in *Ante-Nicene Fathers*, 1:550. Brackets added.

26. Ibid., 3.23.1, in *Ante-Nicene Fathers*, 1:456.

27. Aloisi, "His Flesh for Our Flesh," 41. Greg Allison also suggests that Aulen has done a disservice to Irenaeus: "he reinterpreted the recapitulation theory of Irenaeus and the penal substitutionary theory of Martin Luther so that they agreed with his position." "History of the Doctrine of the Atonement," 16.

28. So argues Mark Jeffrey Olson in *Irenaeus, the Valentinian Gnostics, and the Kingdom of God*, 88. Cited in Aloisi, "His Flesh for Our Flesh," 41.

by faith and effects an ethical transformation in their lives, and by his obedience compensates for the disobedience of Adam."[29] Irenaeus held that Christ recapitulated every aspect of human experience so as to effect the reversal of the curse:

> Wherefore also He passed through every stage of life, restoring to all communion with God. . . . For it behooved Him who was to destroy sin, and redeem man under the power of death, that He should Himself be made that very same thing which he was, that is, man; who had been drawn by sin into bondage, but was held by death, so that sin should be destroyed by man, and man should go forth from death, . . . God recapitulated in Himself the ancient formation of man, that He might kill sin, deprive death of its power, and vivify man; and therefore His works are true.[30]

Irenaeus did not view the plight of humanity solely in terms of being victimized by Satan, then. He also understood man to be under the bondage of his own sin, and subject to the death his own sin introduced. He also held that man's sin places him in God's "debt," and that this debt could only be paid off "by means of a tree."[31] He goes on: "By transgressing [God's] commandment, we became his enemies. And therefore in the last times the Lord has restored us into friendship through His incarnation, having become 'the Mediator between God and men;' propitiating indeed for us the Father against whom we had sinned, and cancelling our disobedience by His own obedience; conferring also upon us the gift of communion with, and subjection to, our Maker."[32] And, invoking the words of Clement, he says, "The Lord thus has redeemed us through His own blood, giving His soul for our souls, and His flesh for our flesh."[33]

Thus, while Irenaeus certainly saw the human plight in terms of bondage to Satan, and part of Christ's work as bringing liberation to those under Satan's power, his system was also more complex than that. He also understood humanity's plight to be caused by its own voluntary transgression of God's law, a decision that placed mankind in God's debt and turned men into God's enemies. Therefore, God sent his own Son into the world to "recapitulate" the total human experience, to live anew every phase of human

---

29. Berkhof, *History of Christian Doctrines*, 165.
30. Irenaeus, *Against Heresies* 3.18.7, in *Ante-Nicene Fathers*, 1:448.
31. Ibid., 5.17.2, in *Ante-Nicene Fathers*, 1:545.
32. Ibid., 5.17.1, in *Ante-Nicene Fathers*, 1:544. Brackets added.
33. Ibid., 5.1.1, in *Ante-Nicene Fathers*, 1:527.

life in righteousness, and then to die a substitutionary and propitiatory death for man, giving "his soul for our souls" and "his flesh for our flesh," so that we might be liberated from sin, Satan, death, and the wrath of God.

Tertullian (d. ca. A.D. 220)

Tertullian, the most prolific writer of the early church fathers, addressed the death of Christ on numerous occasions. In his third book against Marcion, he writes that Christ's death is the very heart of the Christian message:

> For he suffered nothing who did not truly suffer; and a phantom could not truly suffer. God's entire work, therefore, is subverted. Christ's death, wherein lies the whole weight and fruit of the Christian name, is denied, although the apostle asserts it so expressly as undoubtedly real, making it the very foundation of the gospel, of our salvation, and of his own preaching. 'I have delivered unto you before all things,' says he, 'how that Christ died for our sins, and that he was buried, and that He rose again the third day.'[34]

In his treatise *On Baptism*, he offers a few more thoughts about Christ's death: The "efficacy of the font," he says, is "established through the passion and the resurrection; because neither can our death see dissolution except by the Lord's passion, nor our life be restored without His resurrection."[35] Tertullian also has the distinction of being the first theologian to introduce the terms "guilt," "merit," and "satisfaction" into our doctrinal vocabulary, though "he did not yet apply these terms to the sacrificial work of Christ, but to the repentance and good works that should follow sins committed after baptism."[36] Nevertheless, the few comments he does make on the atonement suggest that he saw Christ's death as an act that removes the penalty of death for sinful men, and his resurrection as an act that guarantees life for sinful men; though, like many of his predecessors, he leaves the mechanism by which these occur unarticulated.

---

34. Tertullian, *Against Marcion* 3.8, in *Ante-Nicene Fathers*, 3:328.
35. Tertullian, *On Baptism* 11, in *Ante-Nicene Fathers*, 2:674.
36. Berkhof, *History of Christian Doctrines*, 168.

Origen (d. A.D. 254)

Origen, the influential church leader from Alexandria, marks another turn in the church's concept of the atonement, being "the first Christian theologian to teach clearly that the death of Christ is a ransom paid to the devil in exchange for the souls of men."[37] In fact, Origin seems to go so far as to say that the devil was the one *in control* of the transaction, setting his demands for mankind's release, which Christ was then obliged to accept. In his homily on Romans 2:13, for example, Origen states, "If therefore we are bought with a price, as Paul also agrees, without doubt we are bought by someone, whose slaves we were, who also demanded what price he would, to let go from his power those whom he held. Now it was the devil who held us, to whom we had been sold by our sins. He demanded therefore as our price, the blood of Christ."[38]

Similarly, commenting on Matthew 20:28 ("to give his life a ransom for many"), Origen writes, "To whom did He give it? Not to God. Was it to the Evil One? For he was holding us until a ransom for us was given to him, viz. the soul of Jesus." At yet, in the end, it was the devil who lost the bargain, Origen says: "He was deceived in thinking that he was able to be master of it, not seeing that he would not bear the torment of holding it."[39] In other words, "the devil miscalculated the transaction. He accepted Christ's sinless life in lieu of sinful humanity, only to find his captive too good for him. The presence of the ransom was a torture to him once he had taken Christ into his grasp . . . he could not bear to hold such a one in his kingdom. Compelled consequently to let him go, he forfeited both price and purchase, both ransom and prisoners."[40]

THE POST-NICENE FATHERS

For the purposes of the present study, the age of the Post-Nicene Fathers stretches from the adoption of the Nicene Creed in A.D. 325 to the birth of

---

37. Mozley, *Doctrine of the Atonement*, 102, cited in McDonald, *Atonement of the Death of Christ*, 142.

38. Origen, *Commentary on Romans* 2:13, quoted in McDonald, *Atonement of the Death of Christ*, 142.

39. Origen, *Commentary on Matthew* 20:28, quoted in Grensted, *Atonement in History and in Life*, 184.

40. McDonald, *Atonement of the Death of Christ*, 142.

Anselm in A.D. 1033. From this period we will consider just three significant church leaders.

Athanasius (d. A.D. 373)

Athanasius, the great debater at the Nicene Council, has the distinction of being the first church leader to write a truly substantive discourse on the atonement. His work, entitled *De Incarnatione*, frames the atonement around a "divine dilemma." Ever since the fall, he says, "death and corruption were gaining ever firmer hold" on mankind. As a result, "man, who was created in God's image . . . was disappearing, and the work of God was being undone." "The law of death, which followed from the Transgression, prevailed upon us, and from it there was no escape."

This was a "monstrous" problem, Athanasius says, which presented this dilemma: God promised that death would follow sin. For God's truthfulness to be upheld, then, sinful man must die. And yet, it was unthinkable that man should "perish and turn back again into non-existence."[41] How would God solve this dilemma? Mere repentance on man's part would not be enough, for God had promised, without caveat, that death would follow sin. Furthermore, repentance cannot "recall men from what is according to their nature; all that it does is to make them cease from sinning." Therefore, the only answer was for God to send his Son to endure the penalty of death in sinful man's place. "He alone, being Word of the Father and above all, was in consequence both able to recreate all, and worthy to suffer on behalf of all and to be an ambassador for all with the Father. For this purpose, then, the incorporeal and incorruptible and immaterial Word of God entered our world."[42] "His own temple and bodily instrument" became "a substitute for the life of all."[43]

With these statements Athanasius brings together God's honor and law on the one side, and the concept of substitution on the other. Sin dishonors God because it belittles his glory; it declares that God is not the kind of being who deserves loving obedience. For this reason, the penalty

---

41. Athanasius, *On the Incarnation* 2.6. Online at http://www.ccel.org/ccel/athanasius/incarnation.pdf. Accessed September 29, 2015. It is worth emphasizing that for Athanasius it was maintaining God's truthfulness, not his justice, that presented the problem.

42. Ibid., 2.7.

43. Ibid., 2.8–10.

of God's law—death—must be carried out. God would dishonor *himself* if he ignored the demands of his own law and allowed men's sins to go unpunished. By sending his Son to pay sin's price for men, God upheld his own honor, answered the demands of his law, and made it possible for sinners to have life.

Athanasius also emphasizes the theme of divine love in his treatise, writing that "Christ gave himself for sinful man out of pure love" so that "in his death all might die, and the law of death thereby be abolished because, having fulfilled in His body that for which it was appointed, it was thereafter voided of its power for men." And, he also echoes the *Christus Victor* model of his predecessors, speaking of Christ's death as a triumph over the devil. However, he does not suggest that sinners were *owned* by the devil, as Origen had done. Instead, Athanasius suggests that sinful men are under the power of the devil in the sense that the devil works to hide the truth from them and "hinder the progress" of those seeking after the truth. Thus, Christ needed "to overthrow the devil and to purify the air," so that humanity might no longer be hindered from obtaining life."[44]

Gregory of Nyssa (d. A.D. 395)

Gregory of Nyssa, one of the famous Cappadocian Fathers, authored "the second important systematic treatment on the work of Christ" as part of his project entitled *The Great Catechism*.[45] Like Origen, he argues that sinful humanity was in bondage to Satan, and that Christ's work consisted of paying "whatever ransom [the devil] may agree to accept"; which, of course, was Christ himself. He writes that Satan accepted Christ's offer of himself since Christ is "higher and better" than sinful humanity, which appealed to Satan's "special passion of pride."[46] Unique to Gregory of Nyssa is his contention that Christ took on flesh in order to *deceive* the devil into believing that Christ was no threat to him. He writes, "in order to secure that the ransom in our behalf might be easily accepted by him who required it, the Deity was hidden under the veil of our nature, that so, as with ravenous fish, the hook of the

---

44. Ibid., 4.25. Athanasius's statement that Christ needed to "purify the air" is undoubtedly in response to the biblical statement that Satan is the "prince of the power of the air" (Eph 2:2).

45. Berkhof, *History of Christian Doctrines*, 167.

46. Gregory of Nyssa, *Great Catechism* 22–23, in *Nicene and Post-Nicene Fathers*, 5:492.

Deity might be gulped down along with the bait of flesh, and thus, life being introduced into the house of death, and light shining in darkness, that which is diametrically opposed to light and life might vanish."[47]

Perhaps sensing that his readers might be uncomfortable with the notion of God executing the work of redemption by means of deception, Gregory assures his readers that God's "goodness, wisdom, justice, power, incapability of decay, are all of them in evidence in the doctrine." His goodness is seen in his plan to save sinful men; his wisdom and justice are displayed in his offering a ransom; and his power is seen in his conquest of death. Gregory concludes: "what is there improbable in the lesson we are taught by the Gospel mystery, if it be this; that cleansing reaches those who are befouled with sin, and life the dead, and guidance the wanderers, in order that defilement may be cleansed, error corrected, and what was dead restored to life?"[48]

Gregory the Great (d. A.D. 604)

The next significant development in the church's conception of the atonement came from Gregory the Great, the venerated bishop of Rome, whose thoughts in *Morals on the Book of Job* arguably represent "the completest synthesis of ancient Latin theology on the atonement."[49] Gregory argued that only a *sinless* sacrifice can truly remove man's sin. Since no one on earth is without sin, it was necessary for Christ to take on human flesh and be that sacrifice himself. Christ did not deserve death, but willingly submitted to death for humanity's sake. In Gregory's words, "of him it is rightly added, *without cause*. For 'he was destroyed without cause,' who was at once weighted to the earth by the avenging of sin, and not defiled by the pollution of sin. He 'was destroyed without cause,' Who, being made incarnate, had no sins of his own, and yet being without offence took upon Himself the punishment of the carnal."[50] Here we have another clear statement of the doctrine of penal substitution, though Gregory extends the efficacy of the atonement beyond sinful humanity to include even the fallen angels—something his predecessors had not done.[51]

---

47. Ibid., 24, in *Nicene and Post-Nicene Fathers*, 5:494.
48. Ibid., 24, in *Nicene and Post-Nicene Fathers*, 5:494.
49. Berkhof, *History of Christian Doctrines*, 169.
50. Gregory the Great, *Morals on the Book of Job* 1.3.14. Cited in Jeffery, Ovey, and Sach, *Pierced for Our Transgressions*, 183.
51. See Grensted, *Short History of the Doctrine of Atonement*, 55.

EARLY AND MEDIEVAL PERSPECTIVES

THE MIDDLE AGES

During the Middle Ages, which span from Anselm to the dawn of the Reformation, a series of significant developments occurred that shaped the future of Christian thought on the doctrine of atonement.

Anselm (d. A.D. 1109)

In Anselm we find the fullest development of the viewpoint known as the "satisfaction theory" of the atonement, the contours of which are summed up in his famous work, *Cur Deus Homo?*, or *Why Did God Become Man?* In this work, which was written in the form of a conversation between himself and a man called "Boso," Anselm explains that what God deserves from his creatures is "the entire will . . . subject to the will of God", for if men rendered willing obedience to God, God would have the honor that he is due and men would be without sin. On the other hand, "the man who does not render to God this honour, which is His due takes away from God what is His own, and dishonours God." This, Anselm argues, is the essence of sin. It is failing (or refusing) to give the entire self to God in wholehearted worship and obedience. And sin demands "satisfaction." Making satisfaction for sin means not only restoring what was wrongfully taken, but also giving back above and beyond what was taken—for only then is the honor of the offended one truly restored, Anselm says.[52]

Like some of his predecessors, Anselm contends that God cannot forgive human offenses without some kind of payment being made. There are two reasons for this: first, he says, to forgive sins without demanding satisfaction would be the same as not punishing sins at all; second, without satisfaction the wrong committed has not yet been made right, i.e., God's honor has not been restored. Furthermore, Anselm says, if God forgave sins without requiring satisfaction, he himself would be guilty of injustice, for he would be treating "in the same way him who sins and him who does not; a thing not befitting God."[53] These things being the case, God *must* demand satisfaction: "If there is nothing greater or better than God, there is nothing more righteous than that highest righteousness which preserves His honour in the arrangement of things, and that is nothing else than God

---

52. Anselm, *Cur Deus Homo?*, 1.11.
53. Ibid., 1.12.

Himself. . . . It is necessary, therefore, that either the honour taken away be repaid or punishment meted out."[54]

But how shall satisfaction be made? "What will you pay to God for your sin?" Anselm's conversation partner offers a few suggestions: "repentance, a contrite heart, humility, fastings, and many kinds of bodily labours, mercy in giving and forgiving, and obedience." Unfortunately, these are not sufficient, Anselm says, because these things are owed to God by nature. In performing these activities there is no satisfaction made for sin—just the fulfillment of our preexisting obligations. All of this leads to a grim conclusion: "if I owe to Him myself and all I can give, even when I do not sin, lest I should sin, I have nothing to render to Him in compensation for sin." How then can a man be saved?[55] There is only one way:

> This [good] cannot be accomplished unless there be some one to pay to God in compensation for the sin of man something greater than everything that exists, except God. . . . It is needful, too, that he who can give to God of his own something of more value than everything which is below God, must himself be greater than all that is not God. . . . But there is nothing above all that is not God except God Himself. . . . There is no one, therefore, who can make this satisfaction except God Himself. . . . But no one *ought* to make it except man; otherwise man does not make satisfaction . . . therefore . . . it is necessary that one who is God-man should make it.[56]

In short, the answer to man's need is Christ. He alone can offer proper satisfaction to God, enabling God's honor to be upheld and man to be forgiven. This is why Christ came. In offering himself up to death Christ earned a reward, because in doing so he went above and beyond his obligations. He did not need this reward, however, so he has chosen to give it to fallen men, "those for whose salvation . . . He made Himself man."

Toward the end of his discourse, Anselm makes clear that the satisfaction owed was not to the devil, but to God: "God owed nothing to the devil but punishment, nor did man [owe him anything], except that, having been conquered by him, he should in his turn, reconquer him. But whatever was required from him was due to God, not to the devil." This represents a significant modification of Origen and his disciples. Man's problem was not ultimately bondage to Satan; his problem was that he owed an impossibly

---

54. Ibid., 1.13.
55. Ibid., 1.20.
56. Ibid., 2.6. Brackets inserted by the translator.

great debt to God. Christ did not pay off the devil at the cross; he voluntarily handed his reward over to sinful men, that they might in turn offer it to God as satisfaction. Anselm's doctrine of atonement is decidedly Godward in orientation.

Like Athanasius, he also seems to combine the ideas of divine honor and substitution, arguing that sinful men must be punished because God's honor must be maintained, and that Christ stepped in to answer the sinner's punishment in the sinners' place. However, unlike Gregory the Great, he did not believe that Christ's atonement benefits fallen angels: "Angels cannot be saved except by a God-angel who can die, and who, by his righteousness, can make reparation to God for that which the sins of the rest took away." But this is not possible, seeing that angels are not like men. All men are united as one race, while each angel is a race of one.[57]

Peter Abelard (d. A.D. 1142)

Turning aside from the views of his predecessors, Abelard proposed yet another interpretation of Christ's death, which is often called the "moral influence theory." For him, the essence of God's nature is love, and Christ's whole life, climaxing in his crucifixion, was designed to be an "exhibition of the divine love" that would awaken men's love for God, leading them to forsake their sins, receive forgiveness, and start living for him.[58] As Abelard explains it in his work *The Epitome of Christian Doctrine*, "Christ's death... was done in order that he might show how great love he had for men, and so inflame them to greater love in return."[59] And again, "Our redemption is that supreme love shown in our case by the passion of Christ. This not only liberates us from sin, but also wins from us the true freedom of the children of God, so that we may fulfill all things from love rather than from fear."[60]

Abelard does make a few statements in his *Exposition of the Epistle to the Romans* that seem to move in a different direction. Commenting on Romans 4:25, for example, he says, "that by dying he [Christ] might take our sins away, that is the punishment of sins, introducing us into Paradise at the price of his own death"; and on Romans 8:3, "he bore our sins in his flesh by paying the penalty for them." Nevertheless, it seems best to

57. Ibid., 2.21.
58. McDonald, *Atonement of the Death of Christ*, 174.
59. Cited in ibid., 176.
60. Cited in ibid., 175.

conclude, with McDonald, that Abelard "cannot be held to be going beyond the terms of his own ethical influence view of Christ's work" here. However he understood the meaning of these terms and phrases, they must have fit within his clearly articulated moral framework.

Summarizing Abelard's views on the atonement, historian Greg Allison notes two distinct features. First, while Abelard certainly taught that Christ's death was central to God's plan of redemption, his view is distinctive in that he rejects the notion that Christ's death has any "necessary connection to the forgiveness of sins."[61] Second, he notes that Abelard "removed the atonement from an objective reality—what Christ accomplished on the cross—to a subjective influence on people."[62] In other words, for Abelard, Christ's death did not actually *accomplish* anything except offering the possibility that men might be internally moved by his loving gesture and reach out to God of their own accord.

Thomas Aquinas (d. A.D. 1274)

Aquinas, the quintessential medieval scholastic and father of the Roman Catholic conception of the atonement, expresses his perspective most fully in Part 3 of his magnum opus, *Summa Theologica*. What his work reveals is a willingness to adopt nearly every distinctive feature of his predecessors' views, resulting in a very complex, if somewhat unsystematized, perspective of his own. To quote McDonald, Aquinas "endeavors to do justice to them all, but fails to gather them into a single comprehensive system."[63] In a similar vein, Wallace says, "[Aquinas] culled from what his predecessors had said about the cross whatever had a ring of truth."[64]

Regarding the necessity of Christ's passion, Aquinas argued that it both was and was not necessary. The cross was not necessary in the sense that God could have redeemed man by some other way had he so desired. He says, "It was possible for God to deliver mankind otherwise than by the Passion of Christ, because *no word shall be impossible with God* (Luke 1. 37)." But once God had ordained that men should be redeemed by means of the cross, it did become necessary for Christ to die.[65]

---

61. Allison, "History of the Doctrine of Atonement," 10.
62. Ibid.
63. McDonald, *Atonement of the Death of Christ*, 289.
64. Wallace, *Atoning Death of Christ*, 75.
65. Aquinas, *Summa Theologica* 3.46.2.

Regarding the "manner" of Christ's atonement, Aquinas argued that Christ's passion operated by way of merit. In other words, through his life and death Christ earned his people's salvation: "Grace was bestowed on Christ, not only as an individual, but inasmuch as He is the Head of the Church, so that it might overflow into His members. . . . But it is evident that whosoever suffers for justice' sake, provided that he be in a state of grace, merits his salvation thereby."[66]

The atonement also served as a ransom payment: "by suffering out of love and obedience, Christ gave more to God than was required to compensate for the offence of the whole human race. First of all, because of the exceeding charity from which he suffered; secondly, on account of the dignity of His life which He laid down in atonement, for it was the life of One who was God and man; thirdly, on account of the extent of the Passion, and the greatness of the grief endured."[67]

Additionally, the atonement operated by way of sacrifice. Like Anselm, he understood the cross as an event that appeased the offended honor of God: "a sacrifice properly so called is something done for that honour which is properly due to God, in order to appease him."[68]

Borrowing from the *Christus Victor* theme of the church fathers, he also argued that the atonement served to liberate man from bondage: "Man was held captive . . . by the bondage of sin . . . [and] man was subject to the devil's bondage," but Christ's work, being that "sufficient and superabundant atonement for the sin and the debt of the human race, it was as a price at the cost of which we were freed from both obligations."[69] And again,

> Although the devil assailed man unjustly, nevertheless, on account of sin, man was justly left by God under the devil's bondage. And therefore it was fitting that through justice man should be delivered from the devil's bondage by Christ making satisfaction on his behalf in the Passion. This was also a fitting means of overthrowing the devil, *who is a deserter from justice, and covetous of sway;* in that Christ *should vanquish him and deliver man, not merely by the power of His Godhead, but likewise by the justice and lowliness of the Passion.*[70]

66. Ibid., 3.48.1.
67. Ibid., 3.48.2.
68. Ibid., 3.48.3.
69. Ibid., 3.48.4.
70. Ibid., 3.46.3. Italics provided by the translators.

Aquinas understood the "effect" of Christ's work to be sixfold. First, borrowing from Abelard, he argued that Christ's work secures forgiveness of sins "by way of exciting our charity."[71] As he says in another place, "man knows thereby how much God loves him, and is thereby stirred to love Him in return, and herein lies the perfection of human salvation."[72] Secondly, he says the atonement has a redemptive effect. This is due to the mystical union between Christ and his church; his passion is our passion, so the price he paid for sins is our payment also.[73]

Borrowing again from the early church fathers, he also argued that Christ's work frees men from the devil's power.[74] And, like Anselm, he believed that Christ's work also frees men from their debt to God: "through Christ's passion we have been delivered from the debt of punishment," Christ's death being a "sufficient and superabundant satisfaction for the sins of the whole human race."[75] He further taught that the atonement effected man's reconciliation with God,[76] opened the kingdom of heaven to men,[77] secured the exaltation of men,[78] and liberated men from the penalty of death.[79]

It is also important to consider Aquinas's perspective on the means by which the good of the atonement is appropriated to the individual, for here his voice is somewhat distinct. On this point he states, "Christ's passion works its effect in them to whom it is applied, through faith and charity and the sacraments of the faith."[80] And in another place he adds this: "it is necessary that those who sin after Baptism be likened unto Christ's suffering by some form of punishment or suffering which they endure in their own person; yet, by the co-operation of Christ's satisfaction, much lighter penalty suffices than one that is proportionate to the sin."[81] For Aquinas, man's salvation is a *cooperative* endeavor in which Christ does a work for man, but man must also work to achieve his full redemption. He must be

---

71. Ibid., 3.49.1.
72. Ibid., 3.46.3.
73. Ibid., 3.49.1.
74. Ibid., 3.49.2.
75. Ibid., 3.49.3.
76. Ibid., 3.49.4.
77. Ibid., 3.49.5.
78. Ibid., 3.49.6.
79. Ibid., 3.52.1.
80. Ibid., 3.49.3.
81. Ibid., 3.49.3.

baptized; and, when he sins subsequently to his baptism, he must perform acts of penance—suffering in his own person, as Christ also suffered.

McDonald comments on this point: "For all, then, of Aquinas's emphasis on the efficiency of Christ's work, it remains inefficient. It is when there is a certain 'configuration' to Christ by baptism and penance that there is filled up that which is lacking in the satisfaction of Christ. True, the work of Christ is the greater element by far; but both the work and sacraments are required for a full legal satisfaction."[82]

CONCLUSION

Because the doctrine of atonement received such little attention in the church's early councils and creeds, it was left open to considerable discussion, debate, and development in the centuries that followed. The earliest church fathers seemed to understand the atonement as an act of substitution, as evidenced by the repetition of phrases like "his flesh for our flesh" and "his soul for our souls." Sometimes, the idea of *penal* substitution was also emphasized. The notion that Christ's passion and resurrection were acts of triumph over the devil and his hosts also became prominent. Then, with Origen, a new trajectory was set as he and his disciples began arguing that Christ's death was a ransom payment to Satan.

The first major treatise on the atonement was written by Anselm, whose suggestion that Christ died to satisfy God's honor became very influential. At the same time, it also met with fierce resistance—particularly from Peter Abelard, whose moral influence theory traded an objective understanding of the atonement for an entirely subjective one. Finally, there was Aquinas, the scholastic theologian par excellence, who adopted elements from virtually all of his predecessors, but also differed from all in suggesting that man's redemption is a cooperative effort between the sinner and God in which both provide meritorious works that bring man's salvation to pass. In the end, of course, it was Aquinas's position that won the day, setting the stage for a later Protestant reaction.

---

82. McDonald, *Atonement of the Death of Christ*, 292.

Chapter 2

Reformation and Puritan Perspectives

THE EARLY CHURCH'S PREOCCUPATION with other controversies left little opportunity for sustained thought on the atonement. As a result, an array of opinions on the atonement emerged during this era. While a number of early church leaders embraced a substitutionary view of the atonement, others argued that Christ's death was part of a divine drama centering on God's triumph over his enemies. Other theologians, like Origen, saw Christ's death as a ransom payment to the devil for the souls of men. Still others, following Anselm, suggested that Christ died to satisfy God's honor; while other men, following Abelard, argued for the so-called moral theory of the atonement. Then there was Aquinas, perhaps the most influential theologian of the medieval church, who adopted elements from many of his predecessors while also suggesting that Christ's death was part of a larger *cooperative* program between God and man to bring man's salvation to pass.

This latter theory of the atonement, which came to dominate the medieval church, faced a fierce response from the Protestant Reformers and their Puritan successors in the sixteenth and seventeenth centuries. While they, too, incorporated many of the elements of their predecessors, they flatly rejected the synergistic view propounded by Aquinas in favor of the idea that Christ's death was an all-sufficient act of penal substitution that is appropriated to sinners by faith alone. What follows is a summary of this idea from the era's leading lights.

THE MAGISTERIAL REFORMERS

The early leaders of the Protestant Reformation are termed the "magisterial" Reformers for two reasons: their reforms were supported and protected by the secular magisterium, and their influence extended to both the ecclesial and political realms.[1] The first of the magisterial reformers was Martin Luther.

Martin Luther (d. A.D. 1546)

The famous German Reformer did not see his doctrine of atonement as representing anything new, but as merely restating the historic faith of the church. In his words, "we are not teaching anything novel; we are repeating and confirming old doctrines."[2] Even so, his work does display a measure of doctrinal advancement. His conception of sin, for example, contains some distinctive ideas. Luther rejected the notion that sin is primarily an affront to God's honor, as Anselm had suggested, arguing instead that sin is a legal violation, and in particular a violation of the moral law as summarized by the Ten Commandments. In his *Lectures on Galatians*, prepared in 1535, he explained the concept by way of personal testimony: "there is nothing in me but sins, and real and serious sins at that[.] These are not counterfeit or trivial sins; they are sins against the First Table. . . . In addition, there are sins of the flesh against the Second Table. . . . I have broken every one of God's Commandments, and the number of my sins is so great that an ox's hide would not hold them; they are innumerable."[3]

This being the case, man's *greatest* problem is not that he has offended God's honor, but that he has incurred legal guilt. "We are the offenders," he wrote. "God with his law is the offended. And the offence is such that God cannot forgive it and we cannot remove it. Therefore there is a grave discord between God, who is One in himself, and us. Nor can God revoke his law, but wants it observed."[4] Making the situation even worse, "we cannot remove [our sins] by works of our own . . . our sins are so great, so

---

1. A tremendous amount of material has been written to understand and interpret the rise of the Protestant Reformation. For a good introductory study, see Spitz, ed., *Reformation: Basic Interpretations*. See also Hillerbrand, *Men and Ideas in the Sixteenth Century*. For a helpful introduction to the theological self-understanding of the early Reformers, see George, *Theology of the Reformers*.
2. Luther, *Works*, 26:39.
3. Ibid., 26:35–36.
4. Ibid., 26:325. Also cited in McDonald, *Atonement of the Death of Christ*, 183.

infinite and invincible, that the whole world could not make satisfaction for even one of them."[5] In his *Epistle Sermon*, delivered on the twenty-fourth Sunday after Trinity, he explained the dreadful consequences of sin: "an eternal, unchangeable sentence of condemnation has passed upon sin—for God cannot and will not regard sin with favor, but his wrath abides upon it eternally and irrevocably."[6] By virtue of our sins, therefore, we all stand before God guilty and condemned. We have disobeyed the divine law and have incurred divine wrath.

This is precisely why Christ came, Luther declared. He came to propitiate God's wrath toward sinful men by absorbing the legal penalty that they had incurred. Pondering the apostle Paul's words in Galatians 1:4 ("who gave himself for our sins, that he might deliver us from this present evil world, according to the will of God and our Father"), Luther wrote, "what are we to do with sins—not only other people's but our own? Paul answers that the man who is called Jesus Christ, the Son of God, has given Himself for them."[7] The concept is explained in greater depth in his *Epistle Sermon*:

> Redemption was not possible without a ransom of such precious worth as to atone for sin, to assume the guilt, pay the price of wrath and thus abolish sin. This no creature was able to do. There was no remedy except for God's only Son to step into our distress and himself become man, to take upon himself the load of awful and eternal wrath and make his own body and blood a sacrifice for the sin. And so he did, out of the immeasurably great mercy and love toward us, giving himself up and bearing the sentence of unending wrath and death.[8]

Luther frequently asserted the impossibility of atoning for sins through self-effort. He asked rhetorically, "if our sins can be removed by our own satisfactions, why did the Son of God have to be given for them?" This represents an obvious departure from Aquinas, who held that justification involves a cooperative effort between God and man in which God provides a partial-satisfaction for sins through Christ, and man fills up what is lacking in Christ's satisfaction through baptism, acts of penance, and so forth. For Luther, such a view can only arise from a misunderstanding of

---

5. Ibid., 26:32–33.

6. Luther, *Epistle Sermon, Twenty-Fourth Sunday after Trinity* (Lenker ed., 9:43–45), cited in Kerr, ed. *Compend of Luther's Theology*, 53.

7. Luther, *Works*, 26:32.

8. Luther, *Epistle Sermon*, in Kerr, ed., *Compend of Luther's Theology*, 52–53.

the seriousness of sin, seeing sin as a "trifle," rather than a heinous reality that "includes the eternal wrath of God and the entire kingdom of Satan."[9]

In summary, then, Luther taught that sin is not principally an offense against God's honor, but a transgression of God's law—a transgression that incurs God's wrath and judgment. And the remedy for sins is not found in personal acts of satisfaction, but entirely in the penal, substitutionary sacrifice of Christ: "On his shoulders, not on mine," Luther said, "lie all my sins."[10] But how is Christ's atoning work applied to the individual? Luther answered that the atonement is applied to the individual through faith alone. In his commentary on Galatians, he wrote, "Christ, the Son of God, was given into death for my sins, to abolish them and thus to save all men who believe."[11] Likewise, in his *Epistle Sermon* he declared,

> So infinitely precious to God is this sacrifice and atonement of his only begotten Son who is one with him in divinity and majesty, that God is reconciled thereby and receives into grace and forgiveness of sins all who believe in his Son. Only by believing may we enjoy the precious atonement of Christ, the forgiveness obtained for us and given us out of profound, inexpressible love. We have nothing to boast of for ourselves, but must ever joyfully thank and praise him who at such priceless cost redeemed us condemned and lost sinners.[12]

A close examination of Luther's doctrine of atonement also reveals traces of the *Christus Victor* concept in his writings. For example, he once wrote, "all those who are in the world . . . are the slaves of sin and the devil, and are members of the devil, who holds all men by his tyranny as captives to his will." But "Christ has abolished sin and has delivered us from the tyranny and kingdom of the devil." Additionally, he said, "praise God the Father . . . and give Him thanks for His indescribable mercy, that when we were incapable of doing so by our own strength, He delivered us from the kingdom of the devil, in which we were captives, and did so by His own Son."[13] He also speaks of the subjective influence that the cross can have on a person. For example, in his *Gospel Sermon*, delivered on Good Friday, he said, "behold his friendly heart, how full of love it is toward you, which love

---

9. Luther, *Works*, 26:33.
10. Ibid., 26:37.
11. Ibid., 26:36.
12. Luther, *Epistle Sermon*, in Kerr, ed., *Compend of Luther's Theology*, 53.
13. Luther, *Works*, 26:40–41.

constrained him to bear the heavy load of your conscience and your sin. Thus will your heart be loving and sweet toward him, and the assurance of your faith be strengthened..."[14] Yet, he did not embrace either the *Christus Victor* model or the "moral theory" as central concepts in his doctrine of atonement, as he did the penal substitution view. In fact, it would seem that he did not embrace the moral theory at all. In the quote above, it is clear that Luther was speaking to those who have already believed; he was not speaking of the effect of the cross on the unregenerate.

Phillip Melanchthon (d. A.D. 1560)

Phillip Melanchthon was a disciple of Martin Luther and the first systematic theologian of the Lutheran movement. Indeed, his *Loci Communes*, published in 1521, was the first theological textbook produced by *any* Protestant divine.[15] In this seminal work, Melanchthon offered his own conception of sin. The doctrine of *original* sin, he says, speaks to our being "in God's disgrace and wrath, to be damned on account of the fall of Adam and Eve." This state is what renders us guilty before God and qualifies us as sinners ourselves: "On account of the wretched loss of the divine presence, light, and activity in us, on account of our blindness and doubt about God, and our perverted, evil tendencies while we are opposed to God, we are sinful and damned." And, while "by special divine counsel sufficient capacity has remained in our weak nature to enable us to perform external honorable works, such external discipline is not a fulfillment of the law."[16]

Like his mentor Martin Luther, then, Melanchthon understood sin primarily as the violation of divine law. And the reason why he saw this as such a serious problem is because he understood God's law to be an extension of the "unchangeable wisdom and principle righteousness in God himself."[17] Sin is not just the failure to be righteous, then, but is an attack on the very person of God. This is why God must judge sin.

---

14. Luther, *Gospel Sermon, Good Friday* (Lenker ed., 11:1–16), cited in Kerr, ed., *Compend of Luther's Theology*, 54–55.

15. Originally published in 1521, this work was significantly revised and expanded over the years, with the final edition in 1559 being roughly four times the size of the original. Quotations from this work in the present study are taken from Melanchthon, *Melanchthon on Christian Doctrine*, translated and edited by Clyde L. Manschreck.

16. Melanchthon, *Melanchthon on Christian Doctrine*, 75.

17. Ibid., 84.

Echoing both Irenaeus and Luther, Melanchthon also explains that man's sin places him "into the dreadful power of the devil," making him susceptible to the devil's temptations, including the temptation to embrace "errors, heresies, blasphemies," and sins of every sort.[18] Thus, he argues, man's misery is threefold: he is a slave to his sin, a slave to the devil who prompts him to sin, and an object of divine wrath.

The remedy for man's problem, Melanchthon says, is found in the gospel. He, like his mentor, drew a sharp distinction between law and gospel. The law serves only to condemn, he said, while the gospel is the news of how we may be pardoned. The law is about condemnation, but the gospel is about grace. "The law says no one is justified. . . . But the gospel has the Reconciler *Christ* and this difference: *freely, without merit*."[19] "The eternal promise of *Christ*, the grace about which the gospel preaches, shuts out all our merit and says *freely*, for the sake of the Lord Christ, God gives forgiveness, grace, and eternal blessedness."[20]

A man cannot be justified through his own external morality, Melanchthon said, but only through faith in the substitutionary work of Christ. "The Son of God became a sacrifice and merited *grace* for us, that is, forgiveness of sins, gracious acceptance by God, and eternal justification and blessedness. The Son himself in this mortal life brings about these benefits in us, so that we are turned to God and born anew; he gives the Holy Spirit and the beginning of blessedness, which will afterward be eternal blessedness in which we will have perfect justification, that is, uniformity with God."[21] "If we believe on the *Son of God*, we have forgiveness of sins; and *Christ's* righteousness is imputed to us, so that we are justified and are pleasing to God for the sake of Christ. We are reborn through the Lord Jesus Christ; he speaks comfort to our hearts, imparts to us his Holy Spirit; and we are heirs of eternal salvation. And we have all this only on account of the Lord Christ, by grace, without merit, through faith alone."[22]

In conclusion, Melanchthon "carries out the penal theory in logical simplicity."[23] Sin, as a violation of God's law, generates God's wrath. Christ, the Son of God, satisfies God's wrath by offering himself as a penal substi-

---

18. Ibid., 77.
19. Ibid., 144. Italics supplied by the translator.
20. Ibid., 148–49. Italics supplied by the translator.
21. Ibid., 153. Italics supplied by the translator.
22. Ibid., 155–56. Italics supplied by the translator.
23. McDonald, *Atonement of the Death of Christ*, 186.

tute for sinners. Man's sins are imputed to Christ, and Christ's righteousness is imputed to man, upon the sole condition of personal faith.

Ulrich Zwingli (d. A.D. 1531)

The eminent Swiss Reformer and father of the free church tradition also understood Christ's atonement in terms of penal substitution, though at times his theological framework leaves one wondering why he felt the need for a penal substitute so keenly. For example, Zwingli taught that Adam committed an actual sin in eating the forbidden fruit, but he rejected the notion that Adam's actual sin is imputed to the whole race. He preferred to speak of original sin as a "disease," rather than actual sin: "An act is called sin when it is committed against the law. . . . I confess, therefore, that our father [Adam] committed what was truly a sin; namely an atrocious deed, a crime, an impiety." But what we inherit from Adam "is properly a disease and condition—a disease, because just as he fell through self-love, so do we also; a condition, because just as he became a slave and liable to death, so also are we born slaves and children of wrath and liable to death." Nevertheless, in an apparent bid to bring himself more in line with his contemporaries (and the apostle Paul), he was willing to use the word "sin" to describe man's inheritance from Adam: "I have no objection to this disease and condition being called, after the habit of Paul, a sin; indeed it is a sin inasmuch as those born therein are God's enemies and opponents . . ."[24]

Though he preferred the word "disease" over "sin" to describe man's inheritance from Adam, Zwingli was also quick to affirm that men are guilty of actual sins and therefore under the penalty of God's law. Additionally, he argued that the only remedy for man's sin problem was a penal substitute, which God offered because of his "righteousness and his mercy."[25] As he wrote,

> [Man's] condition is so pitiable that he is dead, the slave of sin, and of such a nature as to care for nothing so much as for himself. . . . Hence arose endless despair of ever coming to God; for how could he ever hope to be received above who by daily evils felt himself exposed to bodily death, and from a guilty conscience felt himself so removed from God that he avoided coming into His sight? But God was better, and pitied His work, and devised a plan to repair

---

24. Zwingli, *Works*, 2:40–41.
25. Stephens, *Theology of Huldrych Zwingli*, 118.

so serious a misfortune. Since His justice, being inviolably sacred, had to remain as intact and unshaken as His mercy, and since man was indeed in need of mercy but wholly amenable to God's justice, divine goodness found a way to satisfy justice and yet to be allowed to open wide the arms of mercy without detriment to justice.... God is alike just and merciful, though with a leaning towards mercy (for His tender mercies are over all the rest of His works), yet His justice has to be satisfied that His wrath may be appeased.[26]

These same themes appear again in his *Exposition of the Christian Faith*, written to King Francis I of France shortly before his death:

> Since, therefore, God is righteous, His righteousness must receive satisfaction for my sins. Since He is merciful, I must not despair of forgiveness. I have an infallible pledge of both of these in His only begotten Son, our Lord Jesus Christ, whom He has given to us out of His mercy to be ours. And He has sacrificed himself to the Father for us, to appease His eternal righteousness. Thus we are sure of His mercy and of the atonement for our sins made to His righteousness by none other than His own Son whom He has given to us out of love.[27]

Zwingli argued that Christ's atoning work provided all that was needed for man to be reconciled to God: "The restoration, satisfaction, and expiation necessary to our guilt has been obtained in God's sight through Christ alone having suffered for us. For 'he is the propitiation for our sins: and not for ours only, but also for the sins of the whole world.'"[28]

On the question of how Christ's work is appropriated to the individual, Zwingli offered the same answer as his reforming contemporaries: it is received through faith alone. He wrote, "Since, then, He has given satisfaction for sin, who, pray, become partakers of that satisfaction and redemption? Let us hear His own words: 'He that believeth on me,' that is, 'that trusteth in me, that leaneth on me, hath everlasting life.'"[29] And in another place, "I believe that remission of sins is surely granted to man through faith every time he prays for it to God through Christ . . . and I have said that sins are

---

26. Zwingli, *Works*, 3:100.
27. Ibid., 2:253.
28. Ibid., 2:264.
29. Ibid.

remitted through faith, by which I mean to say that faith alone makes a man sure of the remission of his wrongdoings."[30]

In summary, while Zwingli's perspective on original sin may have diverged a bit from his Protestant contemporaries, his basic conception of the atoning work of Christ was on par with them. Like them, he defined sin as a violation of the divine law. Like them, he affirmed that the only remedy for man's problem was a penal substitute. Like them, he believed that the payment for sins made by that substitute, Christ, is received by faith alone.

John Calvin (d. A.D. 1564)

The great Genevan Reformer and father of the Reformed tradition had a multifaceted perspective on the atonement, with the main emphasis of his doctrine being the idea of penal substitution.[31] What distinguished Calvin's perspective from his Lutheran contemporaries was his decision to "locate the penal substitutionary atonement within Christ's larger work of prophet, king, and priest."[32] This is because, for Calvin, the threefold office of Christ is what qualified him to serve as man's redeemer.[33]

Calvin explained man's need for a redeemer in much the way that Luther had done. "God's wrath and curse always lie upon sinners," he said, "until they are absolved of guilt. Since [God] is a righteous Judge, he does not allow his law to be broken without punishment, but is equipped to avenge it."[34] This should not be interpreted to mean that God has *only* wrath toward sinful man, Calvin argued, for the Scriptures reveal that God also has a profound love for humanity. Indeed, it is because of his love that God sent his Son to deal with man's sin problem.[35] And it was because Christ came as a divine-human priest that he was capable of acting on man's behalf, "to render the Father favorable and propitious toward us by an eternal

---

30. Ibid.

31. For an excellent summary of Calvin's full perspective, see Peterson, *Calvin's Doctrine of the Atonement*. Peterson disputes the claim that penal substitution was at the heart of Calvin's doctrine, stating that "it is difficult to determine which of the three atonement themes played the greatest role in Calvin's thought: *Christus Victor* theme . . . the sacrificial theme . . . or the legal theme. All three were prominent in Calvin's doctrine of the work of Christ" (55).

32. Allison, "History of the Doctrine of Atonement," 11.

33. McDonald, *Atonement of the Death of Christ*, 188.

34. Calvin, *Institutes*, 2.16.2.

35. Ibid., 2.16.2.

law of reconciliation," blotting out our guilt by making satisfaction for our sins.[36]

Calvin was also careful to stress that Christ's atoning work included living an obedient life, as well as dying a substitutionary death. He wrote, "from the time when he took on the form of a servant, [Christ] began to pay the price of liberation in order to redeem us," though our salvation is "especially and properly" owing to Christ's death.[37]

Calvin further stressed the importance of the *manner* in which Christ died. It had to be "a form of death . . . in which he might free us both by transferring our condemnation to himself and by taking our guilt upon himself." Such was only possible through the cross, he declared: "The cross was accursed, not only in human opinion but by decree of God's law [Deut 21:23]. Hence, when Christ is hanged upon the cross, he makes himself subject to the curse. It had to happen in this way in order that the whole curse—which on account of our sins awaited us, or rather lay upon us—might be lifted from us, while it was transferred to him."[38]

In one particularly vivid passage, Calvin explained both the plight of humanity and the subsequent blessings secured through Christ's work. He wrote,

> [Mankind] was estranged from God through sin, is an heir of wrath, subject to the curse of eternal death, excluded from all hope of salvation, beyond every blessing of God, the slave of Satan, captive under the yoke of sin, destined finally for a dreadful destruction and already involved in it; and that at this point Christ interceded as his advocate, took upon himself and suffered the punishment that, from God's righteous judgment, threatened all sinners; that he purged with his blood those evils which had rendered sinners hateful to God; that by this expiation he made satisfaction and sacrifice duly to God the Father; that as intercessor he has appeased God's wrath; that on this foundation rests the peace of God with men; that by this bond his benevolence is maintained toward them."[39]

"This is our acquittal," Calvin says: "the guilt that held us liable for punishment has been transferred to the head of the Son of God [Isa 53:12].

---

36. Ibid., 2.15.6.
37. Ibid., 2.16.5.
38. Ibid., 2.16.6.
39. Ibid., 2.16.2.

We must, above all, remember this substitution, lest we tremble and remain anxious throughout life—as if God's righteous vengeance, which the Son of God has taken upon himself, still hung over us."[40]

THE ENGLISH PURITANS

Joel Beeke and Mark Jones explain that "the word 'Puritan' originated in the 1560s as a bit of pejorative hurled at people who wanted further reformation in the Church of England," who wanted to bring the church into greater conformity with the Word of God.[41] While enjoying some measure of theological diversity, this movement largely borrowed from the Reformed orthodox tradition. Three Puritans in particular stand out for their contributions to the Reformed orthodox perspective on the atonement: William Ames, John Owen, and John Flavel.

William Ames (d. A.D. 1633)

William Ames, a disciple of William Perkins and a prominent figure in the Congregationalist movement, spent much of his ministry in the Netherlands. His *Medulla Theologica*, a work of systematic theology first published in 1623, "held sway as a clear, persuasive expression of Puritan belief and practice,"[42] particularly in New England, for many decades. It was the standard text at Harvard and Yale and was studied meticulously by Jonathan Edwards, whose copy is brimming with marginal notes.[43]

In this work, Ames sets his doctrine of atonement in the context of his covenant theology. Adam, the father of the human race, was under a covenant of works in the garden of Eden, standing as the representative of all men. When he sinned, he was expressing his contempt for that covenant.[44] As a result, all humanity is now under the curse of that breached covenant. This has produced a twofold consequence: "first, guilt and a sense of wickedness, [and] second, punishment."[45]

---

40. Ibid., 2.16.5.
41. Beeke and Jones, *Puritan Theology*, 1.
42. Eusden, "Introduction," in Ames, *Marrow of Theology*, 1.
43. Eusden, *Puritans, Lawyers, and Politics*, 191.
44. Ames, *Marrow of Theology*, 114.
45. Ibid., 116–17.

God's punishment for sin is death, Ames said, which involves *both* the forfeiture of life and "subjection to misery." This misery includes estrangement from God; bondage to sin, Satan, and the world; and eternal judgment.[46] The only way to be liberated from this dreadful punishment would be to have a "mediator" step in "to intercede between God and man making perfect reconciliation between them." And the only one who could fulfill this role was Christ.[47]

Ames, like Calvin, set Christ's mediatorial work within the context of his threefold office of prophet, priest, and king. As priest, Christ was able to provide expiation for man's sins by offering a sacrifice. The sacrifice that Christ offered was, of course, himself: "Christ was the priest, the sacrifice, and the altar." Key to the acceptability of his self-sacrifice was his unique position as the God-man: "if he had not been man, he would not have been a fitting sacrifice; and if he had not been God, the sacrifice would not have been sufficient."[48]

As a proper sacrifice for sins, Christ took upon himself the exact punishment that his people would have been obliged to endure, which is to say that his sufferings "equaled all the misery which the sins of men deserved"[49] and was "the same in kind and proportion as the death justly due for the sins of men. It corresponded in degree, parts, and kind."[50]

In the twentieth chapter of book 1 of his *Medulla Theologica*, Ames also explained what he meant when he said that Christ's sacrifice made "satisfaction" for sins. Echoing the thought of Anselm, he explained that the Scriptures call Christ's work a satisfaction "because it is for the honor of God as a kind of recompense for the injury done to him by our sins."[51] Additionally, it is called satisfaction because Christ's work earned "merit" for his people, which is the basis for their new righteous standing before God; though he is careful not to draw too hard a distinction between satisfaction and merit, saying, "the achievements of merit and satisfaction by Christ do not differ essentially, in such a way as to be identified in different actions; they are two phases of one and the same obedience." Finally, regarding the manner and extent of the atonement's application, Ames argued that the benefits of

---

46. Ibid., 119–20.
47. Ibid., 129.
48. Ibid., 133.
49. Ibid.
50. Ibid., 142.
51. Ibid., 135.

Christ's work are received through the supernatural operation of the Holy Spirit, "to all those and only those for whom it was obtained by the intention of Christ and the Father."[52]

In Ames, then, we see the confluence of several different concepts relating to the doctrine of atonement. Most noteworthy, perhaps, is his twofold understanding of Christ's satisfaction, which brings together the ideas of Anselm and the Protestant Reformers. He says, first, that Christ satisfied God's *honor*, which was injured by sin; and second, that he satisfied the demands of God's *retributive justice*, which required punishment for sin. This strongly suggests that Ames saw the concepts of divine honor and divine justice in the atonement to be complimentary, not contradictory. The two concepts seem to have come together for Ames in this manner: for him, God's "honor" includes both his position and his righteousness. This is indicated by Ames's use of Romans 3:25. He writes, "[Christ's work] is called satisfaction because it is for the honor of God as a kind of recompense for the injury done to him by our sins. Rom. 3:25, 'Whom God set forth . . . to show his righteousness.'"[53] And God's righteousness, according to Ames, is his perfect character, which is displayed in his readiness to judge sin and justify the righteous. This is indicated when he says, in the same paragraph as the previous statement, "Satisfaction takes away condemnation, Rom. 8:34, and finally brings with it reconciliation to salvation, Rom. 5:10."[54] So God's honor includes his righteousness, and his righteousness is that which demands that those who sin against him face condemnation. In saying that Christ died to *satisfy* God's honor, then, Ames is saying that Christ died to answer God's person and position. Or, to borrow the language of the passage Ames cites, Christ died to pay the full penalty that God's righteousness demands for men's sins, so that God might be just, and the justifier of the one who has faith in Christ. Thus, Christ's dying to satisfy God's *honor*, and his dying as a *penal substitute* for sinners, are merged into one in Ames's thought.

John Owen (d. A.D. 1683)

John Owen, another prominent representative of Edwards's Congregationalist heritage, is judged by some to be England's greatest theologian.[55] In

---

52. Ibid., 150.
53. Ibid., 135.
54. Ibid.
55. Jeffery, Ovey, and Sach make this claim, for example, in *Pierced for Our*

one of his more famous works, *The Death of Death in the Death of Christ*,[56] Owen "made a signal contribution to, and [had a] permanent influence upon, the doctrine of atonement."[57] The book was written as a polemic against the doctrine of universal redemption, arguing forcefully that Christ's death was intended for the elect alone. Regarding the question of how Christ's death accomplishes their salvation, Owen answered, like his Reformation forebears, that Christ's death secured their salvation by means of penal substitution. This point is particularly emphasized in the seventh chapter of his work. Beginning with a summary statement, he said: "by his death he made satisfaction to the justice of God for their sins for whom he died, that so they might go free." Regarding his definition of "satisfaction," Owen wrote, "*Satisfaction* is a term borrowed from the law ... and it is *a full compensation of the creditor from the debtor.*" "Personal debts are injuries and faults," Owen explained, "which when a man hath committed, he is liable to punishment. He that is to inflict that punishment, or upon whom it lieth to see that it be done, is, or may be, the creditor; which he must do, unless satisfaction be made."[58]

Applying this legal concept to theology, Owen declared that man is the debtor, God is the creditor, sin is the debt, death is the required satisfaction, and man's obligation to make satisfaction is bound up in the divine law. This is where Christ comes in. Christ volunteered to make satisfaction on behalf of the elect. Like Ames, Owen argued that the satisfaction Christ made at the cross was an "exact equivalent" for the sins of the elect in order to satisfy their obligations to the law. He wrote, "[Christ's death] was a full, valuable compensation, made to the justice of God, for all the sins of all those for whom he made satisfaction, by undergoing that same punishment which, by reason of the obligation that was upon them, they themselves were bound to undergo. When I say *the same*, I mean essentially the same in weight and pressure, though not in all accidents of duration and the like; for it was impossible he should be detained by death."[59]

Transgressions, 189.

56. Owen, *Death of Death in the Death of Christ*, vol. 10, in *Works*, 140–428. This work has also been published as a stand-alone volume with an introduction by J. I. Packer (2002). Subsequent quotations of Owen will come from the latter edition.

57. McDonald, *Atonement of the Death of Christ*, 293.

58. Owen, *Death of Death*, 153. Italics original.

59. Ibid., 157–58. Quoted in McDonald, *Atonement of the Death of Christ*, 294.

Part 1: Atonement Prior to Jonathan Edwards

The result of Christ's work is that the debt owed by the elect because of their sins has been fully paid: "whereas to receive a discharge from farther trouble is equitably due to a debtor who hath been in obligation, his debt being paid, the Lord, having accepted of the payment from Christ in the stead of all them for whom he died, ought in justice, according to that obligation which, in free grace, he hath put upon himself, to grant them a discharge." Moreover, "Christ . . . by his death, did merit and purchase, for all those for whom he died, all those things which in the Scripture are assigned to be the fruits and effects of his death."[60] So the elect not only live debt free, but also in possession of a great spiritual inheritance because of Christ.

All of this was accomplished by means of imputation. The debt owed by the elect was placed upon Christ, and Christ's merit was given to the elect. Owen wrote,

> God's gracious pardoning of sins compriseth the whole dispensation of grace towards us in Christ, whereof there are two parts: first, the laying of our sins on Christ, or making him to be sin for us; which was merely and purely an act of his free grace, which he did for his own sake. Secondly, the gracious imputation of the righteousness of Christ to us, or making us the righteousness of God in him; which is no less of grace and mercy, and that because the very merit of Christ himself hath its foundation in a free compact and covenant. However, that remission, grace, and pardon, which is in God for sinners, is not opposed to Christ's merits, but ours. He pardoneth all to us; but he spared not his only Son, he bated not one farthing. . . . Remission, then, excludes not a full satisfaction by the solution of the very thing in the obligation, but only the solution or satisfaction by him to whom pardon and remission are granted. So that notwithstanding anything said to the contrary, the death of Christ made satisfaction in the very thing that is required in the obligation. He took away the curse, by 'being made a curse' (Gal. 3:13). He delivered us from sin, being 'made sin' (2 Cor. 5:21). He underwent death, that we might be delivered from death . . . reparation was made unto God, and satisfaction given for all the detriment that might accrue to him by the sin and rebellion of them for whom this satisfaction was made.[61]

McDonald concludes: "For Owen, then, Christ's death is the full satisfaction for the sins of God's redeemed. His death has satisfied the

---

60. Ibid., 175. Quoted in McDonald, *Atonement of the Death of Christ*, 295.
61. Ibid., 156–57. Quoted in McDonald, *Atonement of the Death of Christ*, 296.

requirements of justice, and by his death those who believe are freed from the wrath of God and the desert of death."[62] In the words of Jeffery, Ovey, and Sach, "It is hard to imagine a clearer affirmation of the doctrine of penal substitution."[63]

John Flavel (d. A.D. 1691)

John Flavel is another English Puritan whose writings are frequently cited in the Edwards corpus. His influential work *The Fountain of Life* consists of forty-two sermons contemplating the person and work of Christ.[64] Like Ames, Flavel wed his doctrine of atonement to his covenant theology, seeing the atonement as the historical outworking of the eternal covenant of redemption ratified by the Father and Son before the world began.[65] And, like his Reformed contemporaries, he also emphasized the threefold office of Christ as prophet, priest, and king, placing Christ's atoning work specifically in the context of his priestly office.[66]

In the sermon entitled "A Vindication of the Satisfaction of Christ," based on Galatians 3:13, his understanding of Christ's atonement is revealed. He began the sermon by explaining that all humanity is under the curse of the law, which is to say that the sentence of death is upon all. And no one can deliver himself from this dreadful curse. "No reformation nor repentance can loose the guilty sinner; for it requires for its reparation that which no mere creature can give, even an infinite satisfaction."[67]

This is precisely what Christ, the God-man, provided. He came to earth to pay sin's full price "in the room of the sinner." Flavel explained that Christ was not made "the very curse itself, changed into a curse," any more than Christ's "divine nature was converted into flesh" at the incarnation. But rather, just as Christ added a human nature to his divine nature, so too did Christ take upon himself humanity's curse. "Our sin was imputed to our surety, and laid upon him for satisfaction." It was "a substitution of one, in the place and stead of another."[68]

---

62. McDonald, *Atonement of the Death of Christ*, 295.
63. Jeffery, Ovey, and Sach, *Pierced for Our Transgressions*, 191.
64. See Flavel, *Works*, vol. 1.
65. *Fountain of Life*, in Flavel, *Works*, 1:52–62.
66. Ibid., 1:154–65.
67. Ibid., 1:177.
68. Ibid., 1:177–78.

Here is how Flavel understood the term "satisfaction": "satisfaction is the act of Christ, God-man, presenting himself as our surety in obedience to God and love to us; to do and to suffer all that the law required of us: thereby freeing us from the wrath and curse due to us for sins." If Christ had died in any other way than "as our surety, in our stead, as well as for our good," Flavel said, then Christ's death would have "signified nothing to us." "For how could our sins be laid on him, but as he stood in our stead? Or his righteousness imputed to us, but as he was our surety, performing it in our place." To deny this doctrine is "to lose the corner-stone of our justification, and overthrow the very pillar which supports our faith, comfort and salvation."[69]

Flavel was careful to stress both the active *and* passive obedience of Christ as the basis for the believer's justification, arguing that Christ's twofold obedience answers the twofold obligation of humanity, which is "to do what God requires" and "to suffer what he hath threatened for obedience." Therefore, "Christ comes under the commandment of the law, to fulfil it actively, Matth. iii. 15., and under the malediction of the law, to satisfy it passively." The result is "our freedom, ransom, or deliverance from the wrath and curse due to us for our sins . . . not only a possibility that we might be redeemed and pardoned, but a right whereby to be so."[70]

THE EARLY PROTESTANT CONFESSIONS

A survey of the doctrine of atonement among the continental and English Reformers would not be complete without a brief survey of the confessions of faith that they produced, for these documents established the doctrinal boundaries for vast swaths of Protestantism in the succeeding decades. While the following list does not claim to be exhaustive, it does offer further confirmation that the Reformers and their Puritan successors universally held the penal substitution theory.

The Belgic Confession (A.D. 1561)

The Belgic Confession, adopted by the Reformed Synod of Emden in 1571 and by the Synod of Dort in 1619, states,

69. Ibid., 1:178–80.
70. Ibid., 1:180–81.

Reformation and Puritan Perspectives

> We believe that God, who is perfectly merciful and also perfectly just, sent his Son to assume that nature in which the disobedience was committed, to make satisfaction in the same, and to bear the punishment of sin by his most bitter passion and death. God therefore manifested his justice against his Son when he laid our iniquities upon him, and poured forth his mercy and goodness on us, who were guilty and worthy of damnation, out of mere and perfect love, giving his Son unto death for us, and raising him for our justification, that through him we might obtain immortality and life eternal.[71]

The Westminster Confession (A.D. 1647), the Savoy Declaration (A.D. 1658), and the London Baptist Confession (A.D. 1688)

The Westminster Confession was prepared by the Westminster Assembly and subsequently adopted by the Presbyterians. The Savoy Declaration, written for Congregationalists, and the London Confession, written for Baptists, borrowed the wording of the Westminster Confession to such an extent that their articles on the person and work of Christ are virtually identical to the Westminster Confession. Thus, only the statement of the Westminster Confession is here offered:

> This office the Lord Jesus did most willingly undertake, which, that he might discharge, he was made under the law, and did perfectly fulfill it, endured most grievous torments immediately in his soul, and most painful sufferings in his body; was crucified, and died; and was buried. . . . The Lord Jesus, by his perfect obedience and sacrifice of himself, which he through the eternal Spirit once offered up unto God, hath fully satisfied the justice of his Father, and purchased not only reconciliation, but an everlasting inheritance in the kingdom of heaven, for all those whom the Father hath given unto him.[72]

---

71. Belgic Confession, art. 20, in Schaff, ed., *Creeds of Christendom*, 3:405–6.

72. Westminster Confession of Faith, ch. 8, in Schaff, ed., *Creeds of Christendom*, 3:620–21.

CONCLUSION

While the church of the early and medieval eras witnessed a multiplication of atonement theories, the Reformation and Puritan perspectives were notably uniform, each of the leading Reformation voices arguing for the penal substitution theory of the atonement. They uniformly held that the law is an extension of God's character, that sin is the violation of God's law, that death is the penalty of sin, and that Christ's death fully satisfied the demands of justice on behalf of the elect. This is "a remarkable fact," Grensted says, "and it is still more remarkable that . . . there was such unanimity among the Reformers in their presentation of the new ideas, despite their great divergence amongst themselves in other respects. . . . For three hundred years, despite Roman and Socinian protests, it dominated the Protestant Churches."[73] In the next chapter, we will consider the alternative perspectives proposed by some of these protestors.

---

73. Grensted, *Short History of the Doctrine of the Atonement*, 221.

Chapter 3

Alternative Perspectives in the Reformation and Puritan Eras

Despite their wide divergence in other doctrinal matters, the Protestant Reformers and their Puritan successors displayed a remarkable level of unity in their perspective on the atonement. Almost without exception, they understood sin in terms of legal violation and Christ's death as an act of substitutionary penal satisfaction. As the Century of Enlightenment dawned, however, a growing chorus of Protestant theologians began articulating alternatives to the dominant view. These tended to cast off objective interpretations of the atonement in favor of the subjective, viewing Christ's death as a penal *example* rather than a penal *substitute*. The most prominent proponents of these alternative views are considered below.

FAUSTUS SOCINUS (D. A.D. 1604)

Faustus Socinus, the Italian theologian who founded the movement bearing his name, was an Arian in his Christology and a Pelagian in his hamartiology. His *De Jesu Christo Servatore*, a "heretical tour de force,"[1] offers one of the most thorough refutations of the penal substitutionary theory ever produced, being the culmination of a years-long debate between himself and the Reformed Parisian Jacques Covetus.

According to Alan Gomes, "the affirmative thesis of [Socinus's] work is that Christ is our Savior because he has announced to us the way of eternal

---

1. Gomes, "Faustus Socinus," 190.

salvation. We obtain this salvation by imitating him."[2] Greg Allison labels this perspective "the example theory of the atonement,"[3] because it suggests that Christ brings men to salvation by means of personal persuasion rather than by means of penal substitution. Indeed, Socinus argued that a penal substitute is not even *necessary* for man's salvation. God is free to justify the sinner by a simple act of his will, in response to sinner's repentance and faith. "If [penal substitution] were the way [of salvation], both the generosity of God would perish and we would invent for ourselves a God who is base and sordid," he argued.[4]

The work of Christ was not to "procure" salvation, Socinus said, but to "assure" it. He wrote, "[Christ] is the 'Savior' . . . in that he announces to us the way of eternal life. He expiates sin by assuring us of God's pardon following our repentance."[5] In this sense, Socinus's theory is similar to the moral theory popularized by Abelard. Christ induces men to seek after God by his penal example, that by repentance and faith they might "receive the forgiveness of God, which he wills to exercise instead of his justice."[6]

Socinus objected to the penal substitution theory on theological, exegetical, logical, and moral grounds. [7] Theologically, he argued that God is "absolute dominus," meaning that he is under constraint to nothing, including the threatenings of his own law. God is above the law. If God wishes to forgive a lawbreaker, he may do so freely: "God is our creditor and we are his debtors by virtue of our sins. But every creditor has the absolute right to forgive the debtor his debt—either in whole or in part—without receiving satisfaction."[8] To argue the contrary, Socinus argued, is "an abominable sacrilege."[9]

---

2. Gomes, "*De Jesu Christo Servatore*," 210.

3. Allison, "History of the Doctrine of the Atonement," 13.

4. Socinus, *De Jesu Christo Servatore* 1.2. Cited in Allison, "History of the Doctrine of the Atonement," 13.

5. McDonald, *Atonement of the Death of Christ*, 198.

6. Allison, "History of the Doctrine of Atonement," 13.

7. Gomes, "*De Jesu Christo Servatore*," 215. I am indebted to Alan Gomes for his method of classifying these arguments, as well as for many of the quotes from Socinus's works in this section.

8. Socinus, *De Jesu Christo Servatore* 1.221. Cited in Gomes, "*De Jesu Christo Servatore*," 216.

9. Ibid., 3.1.221. Cited in Gomes, "*De Jesu Christo Servatore*," 216. Gomes argues that Socinus's views were shaped at least in part by late medieval theology, particularly by Duns Scotus. "However," he writes, "these nominalist influences should be seen as but one of the

Socinus also objected to the notion that justice and mercy are "real attributes or qualities 'residing in' God." "Rather," he said, "mercy and punitive justice must be understood as mere effects of the divine will."[10] In other words, nothing in God's nature compels him to either punish sin or extend grace. He simply chooses to do the one or the other by divine fiat. If justice and mercy were attributes of God, then God would be caught in a hopeless contradiction—being compelled to punish, while simultaneously being compelled to forgive. "They are unable to stand together," he said.[11]

Exegetically, Socinus argued that Reformed orthodox theologians were twisting the true meaning of the Scriptures with a rigid literalism. Specifically, those Scripture texts describing Christ's work in terms of "redemption" are meant to be taken metaphorically, not realistically. While there are certainly similarities between the literal concept of redemption and the work that Christ accomplished, the analogy also breaks down in key places, he said. For example, Christ's death may have been the "price" of our redemption, but that price was not actually paid to anyone. When the Scriptures use the language of redemption to describe Christ's work, then, the idea should be understood in terms of "liberation," just as the term is used in the exodus story, where God "redeemed" the Israelites from their bondage in Egypt.[12] Regarding those passages that speak of Christ dying "for" us, Socinus argued that the term does not mean "in the place of," but merely "for the benefit or welfare of," signifying that Christ died "in order that we should receive the greatest advantage."[13] Socinus also appealed to those Scripture texts which suggest that God's forgiveness is freely offered *apart* from satisfaction, such as God's forgiveness of Cain. He rejected the idea that God's forgiveness of Cain was based on the future satisfaction of Christ, or that God's present forgiveness is based on a past satisfaction.[14]

Socinus was also an early Rationalist who believed that all "unreasonable" doctrines must be discarded; and in his opinion, the penal substitution theory is unreasonable. He argued that the concepts of satisfaction and remission, key to the penal substitution theory, are "mutually exclusive

---

many intellectual tributaries one must ford to understand Socinus properly." Ibid., 218–19.

10. Gomes, "*De Jesu Christo Servatore*," 219.

11. Socinus, *De Jesu Christo Servatore* 3.1.223. Quoted in Gomes, "*De Jesu Christo Servatore*," 220.

12. Ibid., 2.1.71. Cited in Gomes, "*De Jesu Christo Servatore*," 221–22.

13. Ibid., 2.8.111. Cited in Gomes, "*De Jesu Christo Servatore*," 222.

14. Ibid., 3.2.230. Cited in Gomes, "*De Jesu Christo Servatore*," 223.

notions," and therefore cannot be logically sustained together.[15] "There is no need for remission—indeed, remission is an impossibility—where the debt no longer exists," he said.[16] Additionally, he argued that "even if Christ had made a literal payment for sin, that payment could in no way be equivalent to the debt owed."[17] At most, Christ could offer himself as a substitute for a single man. He could not, however, pay the eternal penalty owed by countless millions.[18]

Morally, Socinus argued that it is "patently unjust for an innocent person to suffer punishment in place of the guilty."[19] "The bodily punishment which one man owes neither can nor should be paid by another person." It is "worse than inhuman and savage," he said. If this is what God did through Christ, "He will have behaved in a way which would make the most savage human being cringe."[20] In short, Socinus posited that Christ's atonement was really no atonement at all. Christ was a teacher and an example, but nothing more. By looking to him, men gain assurance that they can seek God's forgiveness and receive it, seeing that God wills to give it to them. But the atonement itself has no objective value.

JACOBUS ARMINIUS (D. A.D. 1609)

Jacobus Arminius, the Dutch theologian and professor of theology at the University of Leiden, did not develop his doctrine of atonement to the extent that "his revision of Calvinism called for." Nevertheless, "he did indicate the lines along which later Arminian theologians were to develop a doctrine."[21] These outlines are found, in part, in his oration on the priesthood of Christ, delivered in 1603.

Arminius set the work of redemption in the context of his covenant theology. He explained that all humanity was "cast down" by Adam's covenant violation, with the result that "God ceased to be the King and God of

---

15. Gomes, *"De Jesu Christo Servatore,"* 226.

16. Socinus, *De Jesu Christo Servatore* 3.2.240. Cited in Gomes, *"De Jesu Christo Servatore,"* 226.

17. Gomes, *"De Jesu Christo Servatore,"* 227.

18. Ibid., 227–28.

19. Ibid., 228.

20. Socinus, *De Jesu Christo Servatore* 3.3.251–53. Cited in Gomes, *"De Jesu Christo Servatore,"* 228–29.

21. McDonald, *Atonement of the Death of Christ*, 199–200.

men, and men were no longer recognized as his people." However, because God is full of "mercy and commiseration, [he] deigned to receive them into favour, and resolved to enter into another covenant with the same parties; not according to that which they had transgressed . . . but into a new covenant of grace."

"But," Arminius said, "the Divine justice and truth could not permit this to be done, except through the agency of an umpire and a surety, who might undertake the part of a Mediator between the offended God and sinners."[22] This Mediator, Arminius argued, would have to "offer sacrifice for the act of hostility which they had committed against God" by means of "an EXPIATORY SACRIFICE; and, on that account, a new priesthood was to be instituted." This sacrifice and priesthood, he declared, could only come from one person: Jesus Christ."[23]

Arminius argued that it was necessary for Christ to assume the priestly office because of the alleged conflict between God's justice and mercy, which he personified in his work for the purpose of instruction. Justice, he said, demanded punishment; not only because of mankind's offense, but also because her truthfulness was at stake. Justice had threatened punishment for sin, and this punishment must be meted out. Mercy, on the other hand, desired to see punishment averted. In the ensuing dialogue between Justice and Mercy, Justice confesses that Mercy is "elevated above the tribunal of justice," but still continues to demand satisfaction.[24]

Arminius presented the dilemma in similar terms in his public disputation entitled "On the Office of Our Lord Jesus Christ." God loves both justice and the creature, he explained. His love for the creature is expressed in his desire to save them, while his love for justice is expressed in his wrath against sin. God's plan for the salvation of men, therefore, required "that each of these kinds of love should be satisfied."[25]

Arminius explained that Wisdom (also personified) "discovered a method" for reconciling Justice and Mercy: Justice would be satisfied by having its threatened punishment "transmuted" to an "expiatory sacrifice, the oblation of which, on account of the voluntary suffering of death . . .

---

22. Arminius, *Works*, 1:409–10.
23. Ibid., 1:410. Capitalization supplied by the translator.
24. Ibid., 1:413.
25. Ibid., 2:221. Cited in Pinson, "Nature of Atonement," 778. Arminius's wording here is noteworthy. He does not say that Christ's sacrifice satisfied the demands of God's justice, but rather that it satisfied God's "love for justice."

might appease Justice, and open such a way for Mercy as she had desired."[26] Wisdom determined that this sacrifice should be a "human victim," though he must also be sinless. Additionally, the victim must be fully divine, he said, that his satisfaction might be sufficient for the "life of the world." Only one person, of course, was able to fulfill these requirements. Arminius concluded, "We now have the person who was entrusted with the priesthood, and to whom the province was assigned of atoning for the common offence: It is Jesus Christ, the Son of God and man, a high priest of such great excellence, that the transgression whose demerits have obtained this mighty Redeemer, might almost seem to have been a happy circumstance."[27] Through Christ, God "gave satisfaction to his love for the creature who was a sinner, when he gave up his Son who might act the part of Mediator. But he rendered satisfaction to his love for justice and to his hatred against sin, when he imposed on his Son the office of Mediator by the shedding of his blood and by the suffering of death."[28]

As both priest and sacrifice, Christ offered *himself* for sinful man "by the shedding of his blood on the altar of the cross, which was succeeded by death—thus paying the price of redemption for sins by suffering the punishment due to them."[29] Through the sacrifice of Christ, God demonstrated that he "hates sin and loves righteousness, and that it is his will to remit nothing of his own right except after his justice has been satisfied."[30] And again, God "rendered satisfaction to his love for justice and to his hatred against sin, when he imposed on his Son the office of Mediator by the shedding of his blood and by the suffering of death."[31] The result of Christ's work, Arminius said, is fourfold: (1) it confirmed the New Covenant; (2) it asked, obtained, and applied all the blessings necessary for the salvation of the race; (3) it instituted a new priesthood; and (4) it brings to God all his covenant people.[32]

While similar in many respects to the Reformed orthodox doctrine of atonement, Arminius's position also contains a number of significant ambiguities. As a result, some scholars see Arminius as a faithful defender

---

26. Ibid., 1:413–14.
27. Ibid., 1:415.
28. Ibid., 2:221. Cited in Pinson, "Nature of Atonement," 778.
29. Ibid., 1:419.
30. Ibid., 2:378–79. Cited in Pinson, "Nature of Atonement," 779.
31. Ibid., 2:221. Cited in Pinson, "Nature of Atonement," 782.
32. Ibid., 1:423.

of Reformed teaching, while others see in his works a significant departure from the Reformed faith.[33] What *is* clear from Arminius's writings is that he did *not* see Christ's work as accomplishing anything for the elect that it did not also accomplish for the non-elect. Christ's work, therefore, while described by Arminius as a "satisfaction," "payment," and so forth, could not have been so in the sense of actually securing the salvation of anyone in particular. Christ's provided a satisfaction for *sins*, but not for any particular *sinners*. While using the general vocabulary of Reformed orthodoxy, he favored the idea that Christ's work made salvation *possible* for all, without actually *securing* the salvation of anyone. In that sense, his doctrine of atonement is more akin to the subjective theories of the era, rather than the objective Reformed orthodox theory. The key statement in this regard was quoted earlier: Christ did not die to satisfy the demands of God's justice toward sinners, but to satisfy his "love for justice," Arminius said.

HUGO GROTIUS (D. A.D. 1645)

Hugo Grotius, reacting strongly to Socinus's doctrine of atonement, expressed his own views in his famous work, *A Defense of the Catholic Faith Concerning the Satisfaction of Christ*. Often described as the "governmental theory" of the atonement, his perspective begins with the following summary statement:

> God was moved by his own goodness to bestow distinguished blessings upon us. But since our sins, which deserved punishment, were an obstacle to this, he determined that Christ, being willing of his own love toward men, should, by bearing the most severe tortures, and a bloody and ignominious death, pay the penalty for our sins, in order that without prejudice to the exhibition of the divine justice, we might be liberated, upon the intervention of a true faith, from the punishment of eternal death.[34]

McDonald rightly notes that while this sounds like standard Reformed orthodoxy on the surface, "when he comes to work out how he sees the

---

33. For an example of the former, see Hicks, "Theology of Grace." For an example of the latter, see Muller, *God, Creation, and Providence*. Robert Reymond asserts that Arminius is responsible for the governmental theory of the atonement, which was later developed and popularized by his disciple, Hugo Grotius. See Reymond, *New Systematic Theology of the Christian Faith*, 474.

34. Grotius, *Defence of the Catholic Faith*, 1.

penalty of man's sin [being] paid and how the justice of God was met in the death of Christ," there is a significant departure from the Reformed orthodox view.[35] Rather than beginning with the character of God, for example, Grotius prefers to emphasize God's *position* as the supreme Rector who has the right to punish or forgive at will.[36]

Grotius also rejected the idea that sin is a direct offense against God. Sin is no more a direct offense against the Deity than a citizen's crime is a direct offense against the prince, he argued. Further, just as a prince enforces the law so that "order may be preserved, manners corrected, license repressed," so too does God. His judgment on sin is not about righting an offense against his person, but about upholding his moral government.[37] This point is essential to Grotius's system. The law is not an expression of the character of God, but simply a set of rules established from his position as supreme Rector in order to promote the common good. When his law is broken, therefore, it is not a personal offense against him, but a threat to the general order he has established.

Another key point in Grotius's system is the idea that "all positive laws are absolutely relaxable." This is because "the law is not something internal within God, or the will of God itself, but only an effect of that will. It is perfectly certain that the effects of the divine will are mutable." Therefore, God "reserve[s] right of relaxing it."[38] Before a good ruler can relax the law, though, he must have a sound reason for doing so, lest the authority of the law as a whole be undermined. Grotius argued that God, the "all-wise Lawgiver," did have such a reason: "the whole human race had fallen into sin." If the law had not been relaxed, and "all sinners had been delivered over to eternal death [as the law demanded] . . . two most beautiful things

---

35. McDonald, *Atonement of the Death of Christ*, 203. Grensted offers a similar comment: "This is the language of the Penal theory, with but one slight change. If it stood alone we should certainly assume that Grotius intends to equate the sufferings of Christ, upon which he lays such emphasis, with the punishment due to human sin. But the inserted clause, 'without injury to the display of the Divine justice,' is symptomatic of a wide gulf of thought between Grotius and his Calvinistic friends. When Grotius proceeds to expand his theory, this conception of the display of God's justice receives a stress which profoundly modifies his whole position." *Short History of the Doctrine of Atonement*, 291.

36. Grotius, *Defence of the Catholic Faith*, 51.

37. Ibid., 53–56.

38. Ibid., 75–76.

would have entirely perished: on the part of men religion toward God, and on the part of God the declaration of especial favor toward men."[39]

This is where Grotius introduces the work of Christ. He was punished on account of our sins, Grotius said, so that we might be pardoned. He argued that while "it is essential to punishment that it should be inflicted on account of sin, it is not essential that it should be inflicted upon the sinner himself"; hence, Christ was able to face punishment instead of the sinner.[40] For Grotius, God's choice to punish Christ rather than sinners is part and parcel with God's relaxing of the law. He wrote, "Who thinks it unjust if, when the Supreme power relaxes the laws, some man useful to the state, but deserving of exile for a fault, is retained in the state, while another freely condemns himself to exile, to furnish the required example?"[41] "There is, therefore, no unfairness in this, that God, whose is the supreme power . . . and who is bound by no law, determined to employ the tortures and death of Christ to set forth a weighty example against the great crimes of all of us with whom Christ was very closely connected by his nature and kingdom and suretyship."[42]

God was not under compulsion to remit punishment through Christ, Grotius said, but he chose to do so for many reasons. First and foremost, he did so because of his great love, which is the chief divine attribute. "God is inclined to aid and bless men," Grotius says, "but he cannot do this while that dreadful and eternal punishment remains."[43] Secondarily, God sent Christ because he "was unwilling to pass over so many sins, and so great sins, without a distinguished example." Additionally, "since God is active, and has created rational creatures in order to give more abundant testimony to his attributes, it is proper for him also to testify by some act how greatly he is displeased with sin. The act most suitable to this is punishment." Furthermore, "all neglect to punish sin leads *per se* to a lower estimation of sin, as . . . the most ready means of preventing sin is the fear of punishment." And finally, he punished Christ because "the reasons for punishing are increased when a law has been published threatening punishment."[44]

---

39. Ibid., 79–80.
40. Ibid., 88.
41. Ibid., 99–100.
42. Ibid., 100–101.
43. Ibid., 105.
44. Ibid., 106.

Part 1: Atonement Prior to Jonathan Edwards

In punishing Christ, God testifies to his own hated of sin and love for the sinner, while also providing a deterrent to sin, causing many to cry out to him in repentant faith. In this way God's order is maintained, the authority of his law upheld, and his worship sustained. Christ's sacrifice was not an exact equivalent of the punishment that man deserved, Grotius maintained, but it was a satisfaction of "some sort" in that Christ's death "met the requirement of God's law as God has relaxed it for man's sake."[45]

Throughout his treatise, Grotius describes Christ's work as an act of "propitiation," "reconciliation," "redemption," and even "substitution," but as the details of his view make clear, Grotius does not actually view the death of Christ "as itself an atonement for sin,"[46] for in his system Christ's death is not a suffering of the actual penalty of the law on man's behalf, but an example of God's *regard* for the law and the means by which he will *endear* himself to men. Moreover, in Grotius's system, "a kind of apparatus of government intervenes between God and man and conditions their relationships." This contrasts starkly with the more personal approach of the Reformed orthodox; and while different from the Socinian and Arminian systems in some respects, it does seem to bear a far greater kinship with them than it does the Reformed orthodox perspective. For Grotius, Christ was a "penal non-substitute," as one author has described it. "Although he suffers rather than the sinner, *he does not stand in the place of the sinner with respect to the penal consequences due for sin*. Christ's death is not a punishment at all; it stands in the place of the rightful punishment due to sin."[47] The terms "penal example" or "moral influence" also seem like fitting descriptions of his atonement theory, given its similarities to the theory of Abelard.

---

45. McDonald, *Atonement of the Death of Christ*, 205.

46. Ibid., 206.

47. Crisp, "Penal Non-Substitution," 159. Italics original. Grensted would disagree, stating that "Grotius adopts whole-heartedly the substitutionary aspect of the Penal theory," in *Short History of the Doctrine of the Atonement*, 294. However, as Crisp explains, Christ's "substitution," according to Grotius, was not an actual standing in the place of sinners; which, in this writer's opinion, calls into question the usefulness of the term "substitution" to describe Grotius's perspective. Perhaps Mackintosh's label, "penal example," is the most useful term. See his *Historic Theories of Atonement*, 171–87, 319.

RICHARD BAXTER (D. A.D. 1691)

Richard Baxter, the famous pastor from Kidderminster, also had a unique perspective on the atonement. Beginning with his understanding of sin, he wrote that "inordinate self-love... is original sin itself, even in the heart of it."[48] As a result of Adam's sinful self-love, guilt and depravity were imputed to the entire race. This was completely just, Baxter insisted, because the entire race was "seminally" in Adam when he fell, meaning that all humanity in some sense *participated* in Adam's sin with him.[49]

The solution to man's sin problem was Christ, sent by God "of his free abundant mercy... [God] resolving to make advantage of our sin and misery, for the glory of his wisdom, love, mercy, and justice," seeing that man's salvation from sin would "glorify him more than man's perdition would have done."[50] To bring about man's salvation, it was necessary for Christ to fulfill "all the Law of Nature, which he was capable of," "also the Law of Moses," as well as all "those things proper to the Mediator, in his Miracles, Sacrifice, Resurrection, Intercession, Teaching, Government, &c."[51]

Christ's chief work, of course, was offering himself as *satisfaction* for sin. God could not simply forgive men's sins, because God had threatened death for sin. Had he forgiven men apart from Christ's death, he would have done something "which is... a monster in government, and so destructive to the ends of his government."[52] Baxter turned to an analogy from human government to explain his concept of Christ's satisfaction for sins. He wrote, "in criminal cases, the punishment of the offender is the *ipsum debitum*.... But if any other sufficient means be found which, without the punishment of the offender, may provide for the indemnity of the lawgiver, and the public good, and this both for what is past by reparation, and for time to come by prevention, that so the main ends of the violated law may yet be attained, this is satisfaction to the Lawgiver."[53] Baxter further explained that while Christ's suffering was not *identical* to what the condemned experience, it

---

48. Baxter, *Works*, 11:125. Cited in Packer, *Redemption and Restoration*, 144.

49. Baxter, *Two Disputations*, 227. Cited in Packer, *Redemption and Restoration*, 141 n. 35.

50. Baxter, *End of Doctrinal Controversies*, 94. Cited in Packer, *Redemption and Restoration*, 218.

51. Ibid., 121. Cited in Packer, *Redemption and Restoration*, 219.

52. Baxter, *Universal Redemption*, 104. Cited in Packer, *Redemption and Restoration*, 217 n. 18.

53. Ibid., 378. Cited in Packer, *Redemption and Restoration*, 220.

PART 1: ATONEMENT PRIOR TO JONATHAN EDWARDS

was at least equal in terms of degree; for on the cross Christ became "a public spectacle of shame, for the demonstration of Justice." Because of Christ's surpassing "dignity" as the God-man, "the remote ends of [God's] law" was achieved by his death, which included "the demonstration of justice, and right governing of the Creature, and preserving the Authority of the Lawgiver." Baxter left unanswered the question of whether the dying Christ actually experienced "the pains of Hell on his soul," but he was confident that Christ did not suffer "spiritual death" (which he defines as "the loss of God's image, and privation of holiness, and dominion of sin and slavery to sin") or the torments of a guilty conscience, or even the total deprivation of God's love which those in hell experience. Neither were Christ's sufferings eternal in duration. But what he did experience was "that debasedness and public shame, and that forsaking of God by the denial of spiritual comforts, and by giving him up to the will of his enemies, and by an inward sense of God's displeasure, in trouble of soul, which was a full satisfaction to justice, or a sacrifice sufficient for God to do what he did, upon the reception of it."[54]

Because Baxter understood Christ's death as a satisfaction for sin in general, rather than for the sins of specific people, he was also a universal redemptionist. He wrote, "[Christ] purchased all men from the legal necessity of perishing that they were in, into his own Power, as their Owner and Ruler, that so he might make over reconciliation, remission and salvation to all, if they will believe."[55] In another place, he explained why this doctrine of universal redemption was so important to him: "Redemption lays the first ground of Christ's new empire.... Upon this groundwork is the whole government of the world built, and all the judicial proceeding, and execution at the last day: And therefore they that deny universal redemption know not what they do: They deny the foundation of God's dominion as Redeemer ..."[56] In other words, for Baxter, Christ's universal kingship was based upon his universal redemption. To reject the latter was to lose the former. Yet, he did not reject all the ideas of the Reformed orthodox. In fact, what he was really attempting here was something of a via media between Calvinism and Arminianism. As Packer writes, Baxter believed that "Arminianism denied special grace to the elect, [while] limited atonement denied general

---

54. Ibid., 390. Cited in Packer, *Redemption and Restoration*, 220.
55. Ibid., 430. Cited in Packer, *Redemption and Restoration*, 223.
56. Ibid., 189. Cited in Packer, *Redemption and Restoration*, 231.

grace to the world."⁵⁷ He therefore sought a corrective to both. Christ's redemption was universal, he said, but the Spirit's work of regeneration is confined to the elect.⁵⁸

Baxter was the first to admit that his theory bore many similarities to Grotius's teachings, yet he was also critical of Grotius on one key point. According to Baxter, Grotius's great failure was his inability to see that Christ's satisfaction was rendered to God *as God*, and not just to God as the moral governor of the world. In his words, "Though I owe much thanks to God for what . . . I learned from Grotius *de satisfact*, yet I must say that in this great question, whether Christ satisfied God for sin as *domino absolute* . . . alone, I take him to come short of accurateness and soundness." He continued: "God is to man, 1. *Dominus absolutus* . . . 2. *Rector supremus*. 3. *Amicus, Benefactor* . . . Sin is against God in all these three relations . . . now sin being the privation of all this, God is to be satisfied for it as such, in all these three relations."⁵⁹

JOHN TILLOTSON (D. A.D. 1694)

Archbishop John Tillotson, the influential latitudinarian Anglican, used his superlative preaching abilities "for weaning men from puritan ideas."⁶⁰ His opponents accused him of being a Socinian, so he prepared a sermon entitled "Concerning the Sacrifice and Satisfaction of Christ" to clarify his position on the atonement.⁶¹

He explains in this sermon that mankind's dilemma is twofold: men are under "guilt, and the dominion of Sin." However, mankind's solution is singular: the self-sacrifice of Jesus Christ. For Tillotson, Christ's sacrifice relates to man's salvation in the following ways: first, though God could have forgiven sinners apart from Christ's work, Christ's sacrifice did serve the purpose of "vindicate[ing] the honour of [God's] Laws," displaying God's hatred *of* sin and man's peril while he remains *in* sin. Secondly, Christ's death provided a way for God to forgive men's sins without diminishing the

---

57. Packer, *Redemption and Restoration*, 230.
58. Ibid., 231.
59. Cited in Packer, *Redemption and Restoration*, 224.
60. McClenahan, *Jonathan Edwards and Justification by Faith*, 77. I am indebted to McClenahan for his work on Tillotson's doctrine of atonement. My own summary of Tillotson's perspective relies on his citations and basic outline.
61. Ibid., 79.

"horror and hatred" of sin. In other words, had God forgiven sins without Christ's public sacrifice, men may have found no incentive to forsake their sins. Thirdly, Christ's death represented God's "gracious condescension" in providing "Expiation of Sin."[62]

Here again, we see an emphasis on the subjective at the expense of the objective with regard to the atonement. Christ serves as a penal example, but not as a penal substitute. Interestingly, in several of these theories, including Tillotson's, we also see a recasting of the concept of "honor" as it relates to the atonement. William Ames had written that the cross satisfied *God's* honor. But here, Tillotson writes that the cross vindicated the *law's* honor, which seems to mean that that it upheld the law's *authority*. This is a significant difference. In the first, the cross answers the demands of God's person and position; while in the second, it answers the demands of God's position as lawgiver alone.

In another sermon, named "Christ the Author and Obedience the Condition of Salvation," Tillotson explained how God's salvation is received by men. He wrote, "[Christ's] perfect obedience and grievous sufferings, undergone for our sakes, and upon our account, were of that value and esteem with God, and his voluntary sacrifice of himself in our stead, so highly acceptable and well pleasing to him, that he thereupon was pleased to enter into a covenant of grace and mercy with mankind; wherein he hath promised and engaged himself to forgive the sins of all those who sincerely repent and believe, and to make them partakers of eternal life." So Christ's sacrifice provided the basis for a new covenant between God and men, which he terms the "covenant of grace." And the way to enter that new covenant is through repentance and faith. However, immediately thereafter, Tillotson added another condition: "That which God requires as a condition . . . in those who hope for eternal life, is faith in Christ, *and* a sincere and universal obedience to the precepts of his holy Gospel."[63]

These concepts are repeated in another sermon, entitled "Of Justifying Faith." After explaining once more that Christ's death inaugurated a new covenant, the "covenant of grace," he again turned to the conditions of faith *and* obedience, which he called "easy and reasonable Conditions" that are necessary "in order to our enjoying of this Benefit [of justification]." He

---

62. Tillotson, "Concerning the Sacrifice and Satisfaction of Christ." Cited in McClenahan, *Jonathan Edwards and Justification by Faith*, 79.

63. Tillotson, "Christ the Author and Obedience the Condition of Salvation." Cited in McClenahan, *Jonathan Edwards and Justification by Faith*, 80.

said, "tho' they have nothing of Virtue or Merit, of any Natural or Moral efficacy, to deserve, or procure such a Benefit as the Pardon of our Sins, for the sake of his Son, whom he gave to be a Ransom for us, to receive us to Grace and Mercy; and I think this abundantly enough to make our justification very gracious and free, tho' not absolutely free from all Condition."[64]

Tillotson's position was similar to Socinus's, then, in the sense that both rejected the doctrine of penal substitution in favor of seeing Christ as a penal example. Where they clearly differed, however, is in their statements on the conditions for justification. Socinus limited the conditions to repentance and faith, whereas Tillotson included the condition of obedience. In terms of the general contours of their theology, however, they were more alike than different.

PHILIPPUS VAN LIMBORCH (D. A.D. 1712)

The Dutch Remonstrant theologian Philippus van Limborch, like his Reformed orthodox counterparts, placed Christ's atoning work within the context of his priestly office. However, like Grotius, he rejected the notion that Christ's death fully satisfied the demands of the law in the sinner's place. His objection was based on the following four grounds:

> (1) The death of Christ is called a sacrifice for sin: now sacrifices are no discharge, nor plenary satisfaction for sins. (2) Christ did not suffer eternal death, neither in intensities nor extent ... and yet this was the punishment due to our sins. (3) If Christ did fully and entirely suffer all the punishments due to our sins, then God could grant nothing gratuitously to us. ... But the Scripture teaches us that God out of his own grace and mercy grants us remission of sins in Christ. (4) If Christ has made such a satisfaction for us, then neither could God justly require of us faith and obedience ... as the means of obtaining remissions of sins; nor could we be justly deprived of the benefit of Christ's death, or be punished for our sins ... for God would be unjust in expecting a double punishment for our sins.[65]

---

64. Tillotson, "Of Justifying Faith." Cited in McClenahan, *Jonathan Edwards and Justification by Faith*, 81.

65. Limborch, *Compleat System, or Body of Divinity*, 1:292–93. Capitalization and spelling have been modernized for clarity.

Instead, van Limborch asserted that salvation is grounded entirely in God's loving decree: "the Scriptures everywhere preach the gratuitous love of God, and his most free decree, as the source of salvation, whence proceeded, not only the sending of Christ into the world for our redemption, but also the remission of sin itself, now that the sacrifice of Christ has been offered."[66]

Regarding the purpose of Christ's sacrifice, van Limborch argued that it was not to satisfy the demands of God's retributive justice, but to serve as a penal example that would turn men's hearts back to God in repentant faith: "By the grievous passion of his Son, which he has demanded for the redemption of the human race, he indeed showed his wrath against sin: no effect of which would have been seen had no expiatory sacrifice come between." Had there been no cross, van Limborch argued, there would have been no display of God's wrath toward sin. And had there been no such display, men would not have turned back to him.[67]

A particularly interesting feature of van Limborch's doctrine was his contention that Christ's sacrificial work was initiated on earth (by his death) but consummated in heaven (where Christ presented his blood to the Father to stir the Father's gracious disposition). The manner in which van Limborch writes about Christ's earthly work is also noteworthy. He writes,

> It took place on earth, when he delivered himself, in order to obey the command of the Father, of his own accord, and freely to a bloody and accursed death, and shed his most precious blood as if it were the price of our redemption; which obedience unto the death of the cross the Father regarded with such favor, that he accepted that blood from the hands of the Son, as if it were payment in full for our sins, and allowed himself to be moved by it to bestow on us complete remission of sins.[68]

The repetition of the phrase "as if" in van Limborch's statement is significant. Christ's death did not literally pay a debt, but only metaphorically so, resulting in the Father being favorably inclined to pardon man's sin. As McDonald notes, this sets van Limborch against both the Socinians and the Reformed orthodox in his doctrinal formulation. Contra the Socinians, he

---

66. Limborch, *Theologia Christiana*, 18.4. Cited in McDonald, *Atonement of the Death of Christ*, 202.

67. Ibid., 18.5. Cited in McDonald, *Atonement of the Death of Christ*, 202.

68. Ibid., 19.2. Cited in McDonald, *Atonement of the Death of Christ*, 202.

argued that Christ's death was in no way an "expiatory sacrifice." And contra the Reformed orthodox, he argued that Christ's death was in no way a satisfaction of God's vindicative justice.[69] Instead, van Limborch argued that:

> Our Savior Jesus Christ was a sacrifice for our sins, truly and properly so called; since he suffered most grievous torments, and the accursed death of the cross, and after his resurrection entered by his own blood into the Celestial Tabernacle, and there presented himself before the Father: by which sacrifice he appeased the wrath of God, reconciled us to him, and averted from us the punishment we deserved.[70]

He, like Grotius, rejected the idea that Christ's suffering was equivalent to the suffering that sinners deserve. But because of his mercy and grace, God relaxed the demands of his law, accepting the death of Christ as an offering sufficient to appease his wrath. He also rejected the notion that Christ's work merited faith or regeneration for anyone. If it had done so, van Limborch asked, why does God still demand those responses of us on pain of death? Faith and obedience are human responses, inspired by the cross, which God is able to accept because his wrath toward men was appeased by Christ.[71]

CONCLUSION

As the Age of Enlightenment progressed, a growing chorus of Protestant theologians began suggesting alternatives to the penal substitution theory of the Reformed orthodox. At the heart of their proposals was a summary dismissal of any objective meaning for the atonement in favor of a subjective outlook. They presented Christ's death as a penal example, rather than a penal substitute; a sacrifice for sins, rather than a sacrifice for sinners; an act that *persuades* all men to repent, rather than an act that *secures* the repentance of the elect. They were universal redemptionists, rather than particular redemptionists. As Jonathan Edwards came of age in the early eighteen century, both perspectives enjoyed substantial followings.

---

69. McDonald, *Atonement of the Death of Christ*, 202.
70. Limborch, *Compleat System*, 1:295.
71. Ibid., 1:295–96.

Part 2

The Doctrine of Atonement in the Works of Jonathan Edwards

Chapter 4

The Basic Framework of Edwards's Doctrine of Atonement, Part 1—God

IN THE FIRST THREE chapters we traced the development of the church's doctrine of atonement from the apostolic fathers through the Age of Enlightenment. The goal of these chapters was to provide a historical perspective from which to evaluate Edwards's contribution to the doctrine. As we begin assembling Edwards's doctrine of atonement from his various writings now, we will approach the task the same way a person might approach a jigsaw puzzle: by starting with the basic framework, and then moving to the vital content.[1] By establishing the framework first, we will be in a far better position to determine why, and where, and how each of the various components of his doctrine fit into his *total* understanding of Christ's atoning work. My presentation of Edwards's basic framework will include three parts: his understanding of God and his purposes, of man and his sin, and of Christ and his work. Along the way I will also include

---

1. Rudisill's work *The Doctrine of Atonement in Jonathan Edwards and His Successors* uses the terms "framework" and "vital substance" to describe the various components of a theory of atonement (p. 125). I have chosen very similar language for my study ("basic framework" and "vital content") because I find Rudisill's distinction quite helpful. At the same time, I have decided against using Rudisill's exact terminology because my categories are not identical to his. Under the category of "framework," Rudisill includes such issues as "the nature of law, love as the all-controlling attribute of God, Christ's passion as the whole substance of the atonement, and sovereignty in applying the atonement;" and under "vital substance" he discusses "the necessity, nature, and extent of the atonement." In the present study, I am using the term "basic framework" simply as a descriptor of the general contours of Edwards's theory, and the term "vital content" as a descriptor for the more intricate details of his system.

a few pertinent biographical notes about Edwards, given that Edwards's life experiences and cultural milieu indelibly contributed to his doctrinal perspective.

GOD: THE FULLNESS OF GLORY

Jonathan Edwards is remembered for many reasons, but above all he must be remembered as a theologian obsessed with God's glory in Christ.[2] American theologian Joseph Haroutunian has rightly observed that "even a superficial perusal of the essays and sermons of Edwards reveals a mind passionately devoted to God, permeated with the beauty and excellence of God, and given to the task of communicating the glory of God to 'intelligent creation.'" Indeed, Haroutunian says, Edwards's passion for the glory of God was the very "source" of his "many sided work . . . and the clue for understanding both his life and writings."[3] In a similar vein, Mark Noll has stated that "the unifying centre of Edwards's theology was the glory of God depicted as an active, harmonious, ever unfolding source of absolutely perfect Being marked by supernal beauty and love," and that expounding upon the glory of God "became the burden of his life."[4]

Edwards was consumed with the centrality of God's glory in Christ from the time of his religious awakening, which he suggests occurred in his late teens while he was reading 1 Timothy 1:17. The verse says, "Now unto the King eternal, immortal, invisible, the only wise God, be honor and glory forever and ever, Amen." Edwards's recollection of that moment was vivid:

> As I read the words [of 1 Tim 1:17], there came into my soul, and was as it were diffused through it, a sense of the glory of the divine being; a new sense, quite different from anything I ever experienced before. Never any words of Scripture seemed to me as these words did. I thought with myself, how excellent a Being it was; and how happy I should be, if I might enjoy that God, and be wrapt up to God in heaven, and be as it were swallowed up in him. I kept saying, and as it were singing over these words of Scripture to myself; and went to prayer, to pray to God that I might enjoy him;

---

2. The substance of this section first appeared in my article "Jonathan Edwards: Theologian of God's Glory in Christ," though some of the wording has changed.

3. Haroutunian, "Jonathan Edwards," 361.

4. Noll, "Edwards, Jonathan," 146.

and prayed in a manner quite different from what I used to do; with a new sort of affection.[5]

Edwards described in some detail how his life changed after this experience. He wrote, "the appearance of everything was altered: there seemed to be, as it were, a calm, sweet cast, or appearance of divine glory, in almost everything . . . in the sun, moon, and stars; in the clouds, and blue sky; in the grass, flowers, trees; in the water, and all nature. . . . I had vehement longings of soul after God and Christ."[6] His obsession with perceiving and delighting in divine glory seems to have reached a new crescendo on January 12, 1722/23, for of this day Edwards wrote, "I made a solemn dedication of myself to God, and wrote it down: giving up myself, and all that I had to God . . . to take God for my whole portion and felicity; looking on nothing else as any part of my happiness."[7]

This may be a reference to his *Resolutions*, for beginning in 1722, at the age of nineteen, he started composing a list of personal commitments to God that closely fits the description above. For example, Edwards's first resolution says, in part, "Resolved, that I will do whatsoever I think to be most to God's glory, and my own good, profit, and pleasure, in the whole of my duration." Similarly, his fourth resolution reads, "Resolved, never to do any manner of thing, whether in soul or body, less or more, but what tends to the glory of God; nor be, nor suffer it, if I can avoid it." And again, in his twenty-third resolution, "Resolved, frequently to take some deliberate action, which seems most unlikely to be done, for the glory of God, and trace it back to the original intention, designs, and ends of it; and if I find it not to be for God's glory, to repute it as a breach of the 4th Resolution."[8] Within a year of his awakening, then, Edwards was already relating all of life and doctrine to the glory of God.

In 1726, at age twenty-three, Edwards moved to Northampton, Massachusetts, to serve the Congregationalist church where his grandfather, the famous Solomon Stoddard, was pastor. Three years later, after Stoddard's death, Edwards became the senior minister of the church. He remained at this post until June 22, 1750, when he was dismissed by his congregation following a series of controversies. Throughout his lengthy tenure, Edwards preached and wrote often about the wonders of God's glory in Christ. It is

5. Edwards, *Personal Narrative*, in *Works*, 16:793–94.
6. Ibid., in *Works*, 16:794–95.
7. Ibid., in *Works*, 16:796.
8. Edwards, *Resolutions*, in *Works*, 16:754–55.

difficult to read a single document penned by him during this time without encountering his doxological perspective. This is why so many have described Edwards's theology with terms like "God-*centered,* God-*focused,* God-*intoxicated,* and God-*entranced.*"[9]

In one particularly striking passage from a sermon entitled "Ruth's Resolution," preached in the 1730s, Edwards expounds upon his concept of divine glory with these words:

> God is a glorious God. There is none like him, who is infinite in glory and excellency: he is the most high God, glorious in holiness, fearful in praises, doing wonders: his name is excellent in all the earth, and his glory is above the earth and the heavens: among the gods there is none like unto him; there is none in heaven to be compared to him, nor are there any among the sons of the mighty, that can be likened unto him. . . . God is the fountain of all good, and an inexhaustible fountain; he is an all-sufficient God . . . he is the King of Glory . . . he is a God that hath all things in his hands, and does whatsoever he pleases . . . there is none holy as the Lord. And he is infinitely good and merciful . . . his grace is infinite, and endures for ever: he is love itself, an infinite fountain and ocean of it.[10]

THE GLORY OF THE TRINITY

During the 1730s Edwards also took up his pen to write his famous *Discourse on the Trinity,* wherein he employed both reason and revelation to probe the mysteries of the Godhead. His basic premise is stated at the beginning of the treatise: "God is infinitely happy in the enjoyment of himself, in perfectly beholding and infinitely loving, and rejoicing in, his own existence and perfections," which is to say that God, both essentially and necessarily, is a God of *love* (1 John 4:8, 16). Because God is love, there must also be "more persons than one in the Deity," Edwards wrote, since "all love respects another."[11]

---

9. Packer, "Glory of God and the Reviving of Religion," 86.

10. Edwards, "Ruth's Resolution," in *Works,* 19:310. This example is cited in Haroutunian, "Theologian of the Great Commandment," 362, and again in Haykin, *Jonathan Edwards,* 3.

11. Edwards, *Discourse on the Trinity,* in *Works,* 21:113–14.

Here is how Edwards conceived of the Trinity: God the Father, he said, is the prime Being, who "with perfect clearness, fullness and strength understands himself, [and] views his own essence." In fact, God's comprehension of himself is so utterly complete, Edwards said, that God's perfect "idea" of himself actually *replicates* himself, so that the divine essence exists concurrently as God, and the perfect idea which God has of himself. This perfect idea that God has of himself at all times is the second member of the Godhead. "Hereby is another person begotten," Edwards said; "there is another infinite, eternal, almighty, and most holy and the same God, the very same divine nature. And this person is the second person of the Trinity, the only begotten and dearly beloved Son of God. [Christ] is the eternal, necessary, perfect, substantial and personal idea which God hath of himself."[12] Edwards saw biblical confirmation for this idea in those passages referring to Christ as the "image," "wisdom," "logos," and "amen" of God. "What can be more properly called the image of a thing than the idea?" he rhetorically asked.[13] Thus, Christ is begotten "by God's having an idea of himself and standing forth in a distinct subsistence or person in that idea."[14]

Edwards argued next that "a most pure act, and an infinitely holy and sweet energy" exists "between the Father and the Son: for their love and joy is mutual, in mutually loving and delighting in each other" (cf. Prov 8:30). What this produces in the Godhead is something so profound that it wholly absorbs the divine essence, so that "the Deity becomes all act; the divine essence itself flows out and is as it were breathed forth in love and joy. So that the Godhead therein stands forth in yet another manner of subsistence, and there proceeds the third person of the Trinity, the Holy Spirit, viz. the Deity in act."[15] Confirmation for this idea comes from the biblical witness of the Holy Spirit's ministry, which declares that the Holy Spirit is the person in the Godhead who beautifies, sanctifies, and communicates love. The Holy Spirit, then, "is God's love and delight" existing as its own subsistence, Edwards said.[16]

Summarizing his position, he wrote,

> This I suppose to be that blessed Trinity that we read of in the holy Scriptures. The Father is the Deity subsisting in the prime,

12. Ibid., 21:116.
13. Ibid., 21:117.
14. Ibid., 21:121.
15. Ibid., 21:121.
16. Ibid., 21:129.

unoriginated and most absolute manner, or the Deity in its direct existence. The Son is the Deity generated by God's understanding, or having an idea of himself, and subsisting in that idea. The Holy Ghost is the Deity subsisting in act or the divine essence flowing out and breathing forth, in God's infinite love to and delight in himself. And . . . each of them are properly distinct persons.[17]

What this section reveals is a man committed to historic Christian orthodoxy, but whose mind was also insatiably curious and confident in the ability of reason to fill some of the lacunae of biblical doctrine. Yet, he also understood the limits of reason: "I don't pretend fully to explain how these things are," he wrote, "and I am sensible a hundred other objections may be made, and puzzling doubts and questions raised, that I can't solve. I am far from pretending to explain the Trinity so as to render it no longer a mystery. . . . I don't pretend to explain the Trinity, but in time, with reason, may [be] led to say something further of it than has been wont to be said."[18] The same could have been said about his doctrine of atonement, which, we will see, was inseparably tied to his Trinitarian theology.

GOD'S INTENTION TO BE GLORIFIED AMONG MEN

Edwards's fundamental theological commitment was to the idea that God is an infinitely glorious being, eternally happy in his glory, and carrying on his existence in three persons: Father, Son, and Holy Spirit. Next, he was committed to the idea that this infinitely glorious, self-sufficient, and happy Trinity created the world to *manifest* his glory. Edwards's *Miscellanies*, which contain his private reflections on a host of topics, are filled with entries affirming this. In a 1729 entry, one of many entitled "End of the Creation," he muses about God's "inclination to manifest his own glory,"[19] meaning that it seemed to Edwards as if God's very nature compels him to express and communicate his perfections externally, the way that a fountain cannot help but pour forth its supply of water. In another entry he muses that "God's glorifying and communicating himself were the sole ends for which

---

17. Ibid., 21:131.
18. Ibid., 21:134.
19. Edwards, *Miscellanies* no. 445, in *Works*, 13:492–94. For a word about the dating of Edwards's early manuscripts, see Stout's article "Dating of Edwards' Early Manuscripts" on pp. 60–90 in the same volume.

he created the world."[20] Edwards's choice in wording is worth emphasizing here. God's glory is not just *an end* for his works; it is the *the sole end* of it.

In 1751, after being removed from his pulpit in Northampton, Edwards began a new ministry in Stockbridge, Massachusetts. It was during this time that many of his classic works were written, including *Freedom of the Will* (1754) and *Original Sin* (1758). In 1755, just three years before his death, he also completed his *Dissertation Concerning the End for Which God Created the World*, which offers his most sustained contemplations about God's doxological purpose for the world.

Significantly, in a letter to his publisher Thomas Foxcroft, Edwards explained that his *Dissertation* concerned the "foundations" of his theology.[21] So while it may have been written toward the end of his life, the work actually represents Edwards's theological starting point. George Marsden comes to the same conclusion in his biography of Edwards: "it [is] apparent that the *Dissertation Concerning the End for Which God Created the World* was a sort of prolegomenon to all his work . . . [and] might be seen as the logical starting point for all of his thinking."[22] It is also a helpful treatise in that it not only explains *what* Edwards believed, but also leads us through the *process* by which he reached his conclusions. Stated simply, Edwards informs us that he adopted God's glory in Christ as God's chief purpose for the world because (1) The idea is agreeable to reason; and (2) The idea is agreeable to revelation.

Regarding the value of unaided reason in determining the purposes of God, Edwards himself recognized its significant limitations. Nevertheless, there is *some* value in it, Edwards believed, for "reason . . . may serve to prepare the way, by obviating cavils insisted on by many; and to satisfy us that what the Word of God says on the matter, is not unreasonable; and thus prepare our minds for a more full acquiescence in the instructions it gives."[23] In other words, the insights gained by reason may serve an *apologetical* purpose, demonstrating the reasonableness of scriptural teaching. Without question, though, revelation "is the surest guide in these matters," Edwards believed.[24] What follows is a brief presentation of Edwards's

20. Edwards, *Miscellanies* no. 461, in *Works*, 13:503.
21. Edwards, *Letters* no. 222, in *Works*, 16:696.
22. Marsden, *Jonathan Edwards*, 460.
23. Edwards, *Dissertation*, in *Works*, 8:463.
24. Ibid.

Dissertation, including an explanation of how Edwards's doxological focus relates to his doctrine of atonement.

Arguments from Reason

Reason demonstrates that intelligent beings are purposeful beings. But not all purposes are held with equal value. There are "subordinate ends," "ultimate ends," and, at some point, a "chief end" driving all that an intelligent being does. A subordinate end is a means toward reaching a higher goal. An ultimate end is a goal sought for its own sake. An example of an ultimate end might be the satisfaction of one's hunger, for the sense of being filled is in and of itself desirable. However, in order have his appetite satisfied, a man may first need to buy a field, plant seed, raise a crop, and prepare a meal. These would be the subordinate ends. They were the means of achieving the objective that was desirable in itself.[25]

Sometimes, Edwards says, a subordinate end and an ultimate end will be bound together in a single action. For example, receiving another person's affection may fall under both categories. The sense of being loved by another person may be valuable in and of itself. However, a man may also perceive some *practical* advantages to being loved by this other as well, and might therefore desire the person's affection as a means of attaining those additional benefits.[26]

Finally, a chief end, or highest end, or last end (Edwards uses many terms here), is that end which is *most highly valued* by an intelligent being. While an intelligent being may certainly have more than one subordinate end at any given moment, and may even have more than one ultimate end, he *cannot* have more than one chief end. The chief end is that which drives the agent's entire life. It is the highest value, loved entirely for its own sake.[27]

Edwards argued that God, as the most intelligent being, must also be a purposeful being, with subordinate ends, ultimate ends, and a chief end for all his activities. On the question of God's chief end in creating the world, he argued that reason could determine the answer by looking at the *effects* or *consequences* of creation. What do we find here? The first clear consequence of creation, Edwards said, is that the "glorious attributes" of God

---

25. Ibid., 8:406.
26. Ibid., 8:407.
27. Ibid., 8:407–8.

have been made manifest.²⁸ Secondly, since the world has been populated with rational creatures, another consequence is that God's glory is able to be "seen," "known," "valued and esteemed, loved and delighted in." The third consequence of creation is that God's "infinite fullness of joy and happiness in himself" is shared with the rational beings he has created.²⁹ Taken together, all of this means that God is *glorified* in his creation.

What does this teach us? Since the consequence of God's creating the world has been his glorification, it stands to reason that this is "what moved him to create." Edwards explained: "we may suppose that a disposition in God, as an original property of his nature, to an emanation of his own infinite fullness, was what excited him to create the world; and so that the emanation itself was aimed at by him as a last end of the creation."³⁰ In other words, since the effect of creation has been the display of God's glory, reason would suggest that God has made himself his own last end in the creation of the world; his purpose for the world is *doxological*.

Arguments from Revelation

Turning now to the more reliable guide, divine revelation, Edwards found that his initial conclusion from reason was confirmed. He wrote, "It is manifest that the Scriptures speak, on all occasions, as though God made himself his end in all his works: and as though the same Being, who is the first cause of all things, were the supreme and last end of all things."³¹

According to the Scriptures, God created the world for his own glory, which is to say that God has made himself the chief end of his creation. This is affirmed by general texts such as Romans 11:36, "For of him, and through him, and to him are all things: to whom be glory for ever. Amen," as well as by more specific texts. For example, Scripture says that God's purpose for his saints is to bring him glory, as Isaiah 60:21 declares: "Thy people also shall be all righteous: they shall inherit the land for ever, the branch of my planning, the work of my hands, that I may be glorified."³² And, it is mentioned as his last end for the *virtue* of the saints, as is seen in Philippians 1:10–11: "That ye may approve things that are excellent. . . .

28. Ibid., 8:428–30.
29. Ibid., 8:431–33.
30. Ibid.., 8:434.
31. Ibid., 8:467.
32. Ibid., 8:477.

Being filled with the fruits of righteousness, which are by Jesus Christ, unto the glory and praise of God."[33]

Edwards offers a particularly long commentary on 1 Corinthians 6:19–20, which speaks to God's doxological purpose for all human activities:

> Here not only is glorifying God spoken of, as what summarily comprehends the end of that religion and service of God, which is the end of Christ's redeeming us: but here I would further remark this. That the Apostle in this place urges that inasmuch as we are not our own, but bought for God, that we might be his; therefore we ought not to act as if we were our own, but as God's; and should not use the members of our bodies, or faculties of our souls for ourselves, as making ourselves our end, but for God, as making him our end. And he expresses the way in which we are to make God our end, viz. in making his glory our end. "Therefore glorify God in your body and in your spirit, which are his."[34]

The Scriptures also indicate that human beings have a moral obligation to "desire and seek God's glory as their highest and last end in what they do," which suggests that this is God's own chief end. For example, 1 Corinthians 10:31 says, "Whether therefore ye eat, or drink, or whatsoever ye do, do all to the glory of God." It is even evident in the prayer, "Hallowed by thy name," which is a request for God to extend his glory.[35] Additionally, the Scriptures inform us that the most pious members of the moral world do speak of the glory of God as if it were the end of all their labors, indicating that this is the proper end for all things. Edwards uses the term "venting" to describe these outbursts of praise. A good example would be Paul's "venting" in Romans 11:36, cited once before: "For of him and through him and to him are all things: to whom be glory forever. Amen."[36]

The Scriptures also indicate that *Christ* pursued God's glory as "his highest and last end." This brings us closer to the connection between God's glory and Christ's atonement. Edwards cites Christ's prayer in the Garden of Gethsemane in John 12:27–28 to illustrate the connection. As Christ contemplated the work he was about to perform, he prayed, "Now is my soul troubled; and what shall I say? Father, save me from this hour: but for this cause came I unto this hour. Father, glorify thy name . . ." Edwards

---

33. Ibid., 8:479.
34. Ibid., 8:480.
35. Ibid., 8:482.
36. Ibid., 8.:82–83.

concludes: "On the whole, I think it is pretty manifest that Jesus Christ sought the glory of God as his highest and last end; and that therefore ... this was God's last end in the creation of the world."[37]

Edwards draws the connection even closer with his next argument, stating explicitly that God's glory is his last end in his plan of redemption by Christ. He sees this connection throughout the Scriptures: "The glory of the Father and the Son is spoken of as the end of the work of redemption, in Philippians 2:6–11, very much in the same manner as in John 12:23, John 12:28, John 13:31–32, and John 17:1, John 12:4–5."[38]

This latter argument also explains why it is appropriate to speak of Edwards as the theologian of God's glory *in Christ*. When Edwards writes about Christ, he presents him as the Son of God, the Head of the moral world, and the Nexus of all God's works in the world, particularly in the plan of redemption. Edwards is the theologian of God's glory in Christ because he maintained that God is glorifying himself chiefly through his Son, whose chief work was to make atonement for sin.

THE GLORIFICATION OF GOD IN THE ATONEMENT OF CHRIST

Edwards emphasized God's intention to be glorified among men through the atoning work of his Son with some regularity in sermons, such as this one from Hebrews 9:12: "[Christ] has redeemed those that believe in him to God, by his blood, out of every tongue and kindred and nation to be with him, *to behold his glory*, and to sing hallelujahs to him forever and ever."[39] However, the fullest expression of this truth may be found in his *Miscellanies* no. 327(a), where he writes,

> The infinite love which there is from everlasting between the Father and the Son is the highest excellency and peculiar glory of the Deity. God saw it therefore meet that there should be some bright and glorious manifestation made of [it] to the creatures, which is done in the incarnation and death of the Son of God. Hereby was most clearly manifested to men and angels the distinction of the persons of the Trinity. The infinite love of the Father to the Son is thereby manifested, in that for his sake he would forgive an infinite

---

37. Ibid., 8:484.
38. Ibid., 8:486.
39. Edwards, "Christ's Sacrifice," in *Works*, 10:600.

debt, would be reconciled with and receive into his favor and to his enjoyment those that had rebelled against him and injured his infinite majesty, and in exalting of him to that high mediatorial glory; and Christ showed his infinite love to the Father in his infinitely abasing himself for the vindicating of his authority and the honor of his majesty. When God had a mind to save men, Christ infinitely laid out himself that the honor of God's majesty might be safe and that God's glory might be advanced.[40]

And with this, Edwards brings our chapter full circle. He writes that God's "peculiar glory" is found in the infinite love which exists between the members of the Trinity, especially between the Father and the Son, and that the atonement is the chief means by which God manifests this surpassing glory in the world. Christ's love for the Father was displayed in his willingness to suffer and die for the "honor" of the Father's "infinite majesty" and "authority," which is to say that Christ died to glorify the Father by vindicating his *person* and *position*, his attributes and his government, which had been injured by man's sin. Likewise, the Father's love for the Son is displayed in his willingness to reconcile with those for whom the Son died and by giving the Son an exalted position because of his sacrifice. As the atonement is applied, and those for whom Christ died come to know, value, love, delight in, and bow before the majestic, triune God, God is glorified in the world. This is what it means to say that God's glory was "advanced" by the atonement. The atonement vindicated God's attributes and position, and provided the means by which men may become happy in him as they were meant to be.

CONCLUSION

The unifying center of Edwards's theology is the glory of God in Christ as the beginning and end of all things. This end is inseparably linked to the mission of Christ, who is God's "perfect idea of himself," the Head of the moral world, and especially the Head and Redeemer of the church, that company of humanity which he secured through his atoning work and has been assembled for the sole purpose perceiving God's perfections, delighting in them, and reflecting them back to him, to his everlasting glory. Christ's work of atonement is part and parcel with God's aim of bringing glory to himself in the world.

40. Edwards, *Miscellanies* no. 327(a), in *Works*, 13:406.

And yet, it was also a work meant for the good of the creature, the two concepts being inseparably tied together. God does not exist *for* the creature; the creature exists for him. Yet, in redeeming a people for himself through Christ, the creature's highest happiness has also been secured. Edwards expressed this dual truth quite ably in *Miscellanies* no. 271, composed many years before his *Dissertation*. He wrote,

> It is indeed a condecent thing that God should be the ultimate end of the creation as well as the cause, that in creating he should make himself his end, that he should in this respect be Omega as well as Alpha.... And this may be, and yet the reason of his creating the world be his propensity to goodness, and the communication of happiness to the creatures be the end.
>
> It perhaps was thus: God created the world for his Son, that he might prepare a spouse or bride for him to bestow his love upon; so that the mutual joys between this bride and bridegroom are the end of the creation. God is really happy in loving his creatures, because in so doing he as it were gratifies a natural propensity in the divine nature, viz, goodness. Yea, and he is really delighted in the love of his creatures and in their glorifying him, because he loves them, not because he needs. For he could not be happy therein, were it not for his love and goodness. Colossians 1:16, "All things were made by him and for him," that is, for the Son.[41]

Thus, "In the creature's knowing, esteeming, loving, rejoicing in, and praising God, the glory of God is both exhibited and acknowledged; his fullness is received and returned. Here is both an *emanation* and *remanation*... the beams of glory come from God, and are something of God, and are refunded back again to their original."[42] And throughout all eternity, "the union [secured by the atoning work of Christ] will become more and more strict and perfect; nearer and more like to that between God the Father and the Son; who are so united, that their interest is perfectly one."[43]

---

41. Edwards, *Miscellanies* no. 271, in *Works*, 13:374.
42. Edwards, *Dissertation*, in *Works*, 8:531.
43. Ibid., 8:534.

Chapter 5

The Basic Framework of Edwards's Doctrine of Atonement, Part 2—Man, Sin, and Christ

GOD IS AN INFINITELY glorious and happy Trinity who made the world and all it contains to glorify himself. For mankind, glorifying God means knowing, loving, esteeming, rejoicing in, and perfectly obeying God; or, in short, *loving* him.[1] Man's love should be so great, Edwards says, "as to have the most absolute possession of all the soul, and the perfect government of all the principles and springs of action in our nature."[2] It should be characterized by a "supreme regard to him for what he is in himself," because he is so "infinitely excellent in himself." "If we love him not for his own sake, but for something else," Edwards says, "then our love is not terminated on him, but on something else, as its ultimate object." This is the essence of sin. "Disinterested love," or "pure divine affection," is what God deserves, and nothing less.[3] Disinterested love is the essence of righteousness.

THE ORIGINAL STATE OF MAN

Adam, the first man, enjoyed the state of righteousness "from the first moment of his existence." Some use the term "innocence" to describe Adam's original state, but Edwards seems to have preferred the term "righteousness"

---

1. Edwards, *Original Sin*, in *Works*, 3:140.
2. Ibid., 3:141.
3. Ibid., 3:144.

because it more accurately conveys Adam's moral uprightness. Adam didn't enter the garden morally neutral; he was positively inclined toward God and good. "He was immediately under a rule of *right* action; he was obliged as soon as he existed to act *right*. And if he was obliged to act right as soon as he existed, he was obliged even then to be *inclined* to act right."[4] "His heart possessed . . . that principle of divine love."[5]

Adam's whole being was set in a Godward direction. He "enjoyed noon-day light, the light of the knowledge of God, the light of his glory, and the light of his favour." His will "was subject to reason and motivated by that love to God which 'was the principle in his heart that ruled over all other principles.'"[6] Adam and his wife understood their duty toward God and the consequences of failure, because God "made known to them the methods of his moral government towards them, in the revelation he made of himself to the natural head of the whole species; and let him know, that obedience to him was expected as his duty, and enforced this duty with the sanction of a threatened punishment, called by the name of death."[7]

THE FALL OF MAN

Tragically, however, it was not long after his creation before Adam rebelled against God.[8] While his sin was instigated by a serpent, the culpability still lay with him, his sin being the result of "an upsurge of pride in [his] breast which rendered him prone to [the serpent's] flattery."[9] Edwards spent years trying to understand how a man created in righteousness could have succumbed to pride, returning to this topic with some frequency in his sermons and other writings. His basic answer was that Adam succumbed to pride because, while he certainly possessed sufficient grace from God to enjoy a righteous standing, he lacked that *confirming* grace from God which

---

4. Ibid., 3:228.
5. Ibid., 3:230.
6. These citations come from Crabtree, *Jonathan Edwards' View of Man*, 22. Crabtree cites excerpts from Edwards's sermon on 1 Corinthians 1:29, *History of the Work of Redemption* part 1, sermon on Matthew 16:11, *Miscellanies, Freedom of the Will*, and *Original Sin*.
7. Edwards, *Original Sin*, in *Works*, 3:238.
8. Ibid., 3:228.
9. Crabtree, *Jonathan Edwards' View of Man*, 23. The quote is Crabtree's own summary of Edwards's *Thoughts on the Revival*, IV.i.

was necessary to establish him irrevocably in his righteous state. Edwards implies that Adam could have asked God for this additional grace when temptation struck, and God would have granted it. Adam failed to do so, however, because his "rational will" had been neutralized by the serpent's deception, and thus his appetites were able to run unchecked.[10]

CONSEQUENCES OF THE FALL

As a result of Adam's sin, he and all his posterity were plunged under the curse of sin and death. As Edwards explains in his sermon from Luke 13:5,

> All men are guilty of Adam's first sin. Adam was our common father and representative who stood in our room: we were all in his loins. The covenant which he broke was made with us all, and for us all in him; it cannot be supposed that the covenant that God made with Adam, He made only for his single person. That is ridiculous, for at that rate there must be a particular covenant made with every particular person, in all nations and ages. We might know that we are guilty of Adam's sin because we see that the effects of it are transmitted down to all his posterity ...
>
> But we have something that is more sure, whereunto we do well if we give heed: Romans 5:12, "Wherefore, as by one man sin entered into the world, [and] death by sin; so death passed upon all men, for that all have sinned"; which is as much as if the Apostle had expressly said, "All men have sinned in one man." Romans 5:15, "For if through the offence of one many be dead"; in Romans 5:16, "for the judgment was by one to condemnation"; Romans 5:17, "for if by one man's offence death reigned by one"; Romans 5:18, "therefore as by the offence of one judgment came upon all men to condemnation"; and Romans 5:19, "for as by one man's disobedience many were made sinners." Also, 1 Corinthians

---

10. Edwards, *Freedom of the Will*, in *Works*, 1:413. See also his *Miscellanies* no. 290. McClymond and McDermott note that this general opinion was shared by Ames, *Marrow of Theology*, 114; Turretin, *Institutes of Elenctic Theology*, 1:610; and Mastricht, *Theoretico-practica theologia*, 4:1. Calvin, however, was content to let this question remain a mystery. Summarized in *The Theology of Jonathan Edwards*, 352 n. 48. On the question of how Adam's appetites could have inclined him to sin when he was created in righteousness, Edwards offers the novel suggestion that Adam could have possessed an "imperfection" in his nature from the time of his creation that would eventually lead him into sin unless prevented from doing so by the confirming (or efficacious) grace of God, which God was under no obligation to provide. For a more thorough discussion of this issue, including a Reformed orthodox critique of Edwards's position, see Gerstner, *Rational Biblical Theology of Jonathan Edwards*, 2:303–22.

15:21–22, "For since by Adam came death, by man also came the resurrection of the dead, for as in Adam all die, so in Christ shall all be made alive."[11]

Edwards's most extensive treatment of this theme is contained in the treatise appropriately titled *Original Sin*. As the work begins, he goes on record as fully supporting the notion that on "account of one man's disobedience, mankind were judicially constituted sinners; that is, subjected to death, by the sentence of God the judge,"[12] and states that "the doctrine of the corruption of nature, as derived from Adam, and also the imputation of his first sin, are both clearly taught [in Scripture]. The imputation of Adam's one transgression, is indeed most directly and frequently asserted."[13]

On the question of how God could justly impute the sins of Adam to the entire race, Edwards writes that God could do so because of the natural "oneness" that exists between Adam and the rest of humanity. Using a botanical analogy, Edwards argues that humanity is to Adam what "buds and branches" are to "the stock or root of a tree." As a result, God treats all humanity, stretched out in time though it may be, as a single organism with a single "moral state." For Edwards, the idea that human beings could be found in "exceeding different states, as that some should be perfectly innocent and holy, but others corrupt and wicked; some needing a savior, but others needing none; some in a confirmed state of perfect happiness, but others in a state of public condemnation to perfect and eternal misery; some justly exposed to great calamities in this world, but others by their innocence raised above all suffering," is an absurdity. Humanity, though stretched out in time and particularized into billions of individuals, is still naturally and morally one entity. This is why every human being can be "justly looked upon in the sight of God . . . as fully consenting and concurring" with Adam's sin, and thus receive the same sentence of death that Adam received.[14]

---

11. Edwards, *True Repentance Required*, in *Works*, 10:512.
12. Edwards, *Original Sin*, in *Works*, 3:247–48.
13. Ibid., 3:348.
14. Ibid., 3:405–9.

THE UNIVERSAL SINFULNESS OF MAN

This, then, is humanity's great problem: it is under the curse of original sin. "By original sin . . . is meant the *innate sinful depravity of the heart* [and] . . . the *imputation* of Adam's first sin; or in other words, the liableness or exposedness of Adam's posterity, in the divine judgment, to partake of the punishment of that sin."[15] That mankind is universally sinful and under the curse is evident from many perspectives, Edwards says. There are, of course, those Scripture texts affirming the universality of sin, including 1 Kings 8:46; Job 9:2–3; Psalm 143:2; and Romans 3:19–20.[16] But beyond this, simple observation also confirms the universal sinfulness of man. Observation confirms, for example, that men universally have a *propensity* to sin, demonstrated by the fact that men routinely fall prey to their "bodily appetites, and sinfully to indulge them, and [are] very apt or prone to yield to temptation to sin." This propensity to sin is clearly *inherent* in man, Edwards says, because observation reveals that it is true of men regardless of their geographic location or other "external circumstances."[17]

Edwards acknowledged that men do occasionally perform good deeds, at least in a relative sense, but he also believed that these "good" deeds are no compensation for the evil that men commit. As he explains,

> The merit of our respect or obedience to God is not infinite. The merit of respect to any being don't increase, but is rather diminished in proportion to the obligations we are under in strict justice to pay him that respect. There is no great merit in paying a debt we owe, and by the highest possible obligations in strict justice are obliged to pay; but there is great demerit in refusing to pay it. That on such accounts as these there is an infinite demerit in all sin against God, which must therefore immensely outweigh all the merit which can be supposed to be in our virtue.[18]

So the good deeds of men are of limited value, seeing that they merely fulfill man's *duty* toward God. But sin, being an act of rebellion against the infinite God, incurs an infinitely large debt. Therefore, no amount of good deeds could ever outweigh men's sins so as to give him a verdict of righteousness, for any man who "in any respect or degree is a transgressor of

15. Ibid., 3:107.
16. Ibid., 3:114–15.
17. Ibid., 3:123–24.
18. Ibid., 3:130.

God's law, is a wicked man, yea, wholly wicked in the eye of the law." All the good that he may do is "esteemed nothing, having no account made of it, when taken together with his wickedness," and so, in the eyes of the law, is "abhorred and cursed forever; and must be so, unless grace interposes, to cover his transgression."[19] What makes this point particularly significant is that it not only discusses the demerits of sin, but also gives us insight into Edwards's understanding of the *nature* of sin. For him, as for the Reformed orthodox in general, sin is *lawlessness*.

Sin is also *more* than lawlessness. In his sermon entitled "Christ's Sacrifice an Inducement to His Ministers," which gives one of his more comprehensive definitions of sin, he says,

> Sin is an opposition to the law of God, and rebellion against the Lawgiver . . . it is an opposing the authority of God and a contempt of his infinite majesty. And as it is an opposition to the holy will of God, so 'tis a contrariety and enmity against the nature of God; for his will [is] but an expression of his holy nature, which is infinitely contrary to sin. . . . And as sin is an opposition to God's nature, so it implies a contrariety to all his perfections, for the nature of God and his perfections are not different; and in being an opposition to his perfections, so it is an opposition to his life and essence and very being, for the being of God and the being of his nature and perfection can't be distinguished. And as sin is an opposition to the nature of God, so 'tis an opposition to his works.[20]

Sin is therefore a twofold offense, according to Edwards: it is opposition to God's authoritative law, but also opposition to God's holy nature; it is an affront to his *position*, as well as to his *person*. When he turns to his doctrine of atonement, then, we should anticipate an understanding of Christ's work that answers both problems. For now, though, we continue with Edwards's arguments for the universal depravity of man.

Edwards argues that human depravity is further seen mankind's sins of omission. Righteousness does not just consist of refraining from overtly evil acts, Edwards insists, but also requires positive good. This is indicated by passages like Matthew 25 and 1 Corinthians 16:22, as well as from the fact that man's chief duty is to love God, which is a positive command. Therefore, "whosoever withholds more of that love or respect of heart from God

---

19. Ibid., 3:131.
20. Edwards, "Christ's Sacrifice an Inducement to His Ministers," in *Works*, 25:663–64.

which his law requires, than he affords, has more sin than righteousness."[21] This, Edwards argues, is where so many fail:

> What considerate person is there, even among the more virtuous part of mankind, but what would be ashamed to say, and profess before God or men, that he loves God half so much as he ought to do; or that he exercises one half of that esteem, honor and gratitude towards God, which would be altogether becoming him; considering what God is, and what great manifestations he has made of his transcendent excellency and goodness, and what benefits he receives from him? And if few or none of the best of men can with reason and truth make even such a profession, how far from it must the generality of mankind be?[22]

The universal sinfulness of man is further demonstrated by mankind's "extreme degree of folly and stupidity in matters of religion," Edwards says. He sees this especially manifest in two places: man's propensity toward idolatry, and his "great disregard of eternal things."[23] Idolatry, he says, "is a most glaring evidence of the exceeding depravity of the human nature; as 'tis a propensity, in the utmost degree, contrary to the highest end, the main business and chief happiness of mankind, consisting in the knowledge, service and enjoyment of the living God, the Creator and Governor of the world." Moreover, it is "in the highest degree contrary to that for which mainly God gave mankind more understanding than the beasts of the earth, and made them wiser than the fowls of heaven: which was, that they might be capable of the knowledge of God; and in the highest degree contrary to the first and greatest commandment of the moral law."[24]

Edwards also explains that men preoccupy themselves daily with the cares of this life, but they think little of heavenly things. He writes, "With what difficulty are a few of multitudes excited to any tolerable degree of care and diligence, by the innumerable means used with men to make 'em wise for themselves? And when some vigilance and activity is excited, how apt is it to die away, like a mere force against a natural tendency?" He asks, "how are these things be accounted for, but by supposing a most wretched depravity of nature?"[25]

---

21. Edwards, *Original Sin*, in *Works*, 3:140.
22. Ibid., 3:140–41.
23. Ibid., 3:147.
24. Ibid., 3:151–52.
25. Ibid., 3:154–56.

Edwards also asserts that the depravity of man may be established by the evil character that dominates the great body of humanity. Persons of good character, he says, have "mortified the flesh, with its lusts; they are dead to sin, and live no longer therein; the old man is crucified, and the body of sin destroyed: they yield themselves to God, as those that are alive from the dead, and their members as instruments of righteousness to God, and as servants of righteousness to holiness." Additionally, they are persons who prefer the favor of God over all worldly enjoyments; they "delight in the worship of God, and in converse with him"; they have brought every sinful appetite "into subjection to reason and truth," and have a "benevolent disposition towards our fellow-creatures"[26] If this is what good character consists of, then what must we conclude about humanity? Edwards writes: "I leave it to be judged by everyone that has any degree of impartiality, whether there be not sufficient ground to think, from what appears everywhere, that it is but a very small part indeed, or the many myriads and millions which overspread this globe, who are of a character that in any wise answers these descriptions."[27]

Finally, Edwards establishes the depravity of man by noting how often attempts to promote virtue and curb vice fail to achieve their objective. Think of all the means that God used throughout biblical history to curb vice, Edwards says. Think of the threatenings, judgments, miraculous signs, and prophetic messages—none of which significantly curbed human sin. Think also of the Reformation, Edwards says. How quickly the countries touched by the Reformation descended back into heresy and vice. The depravity of man runs so deep that men continue in sin even though sin is so often "contrary to men's temporal interest and comfort in this world, and their having continually before their eyes so many instances of persons made miserable by their vices; the restraints of human laws, without which men cannot live in society; the judgments of God brought on men for their wickedness, with which history abounds, and the providential rewards of virtue; and innumerable particular means, that God has used from age to age, to curb the wickedness of mankind."[28]

Finally, "the universal reign of death, over persons of all ages indiscriminately, with the awful circumstances and attendants of death, proves

26. Ibid., 3:158–59.
27. Ibid., 3:160.
28. Ibid., 3:187.

that men come sinful into the world," Edwards says.²⁹ Death is the wage of sin. The fact that not even infants are spared from death shows that all are sinners, subject to sin's curse.³⁰

A fitting summary of this entire section may be a quote from Edwards's sermon on Hebrews 13:8. He writes,

> Adam, the first surety of mankind, failed in his work, because he was a mere creature, and so a mutable being. Though he had so great a trust committed to him, as the care of the eternal welfare of all his posterity, yet, not being unchangeable, he failed, and transgressed God's holy covenant. He was led aside, and drawn away by the subtle temptation of the devil. He being a changeable being, his subtle adversary found means to turn him aside, and so he fell, and all his posterity fell with him.

What humanity needed now was a new Surety; one who would not fall short. Mankind needed "a surety that was unchangeable and could not fail in his work."³¹ This brings us to the mission of Christ.

CHRIST: REDEEMER OF SINFUL MAN

Jesus Christ, the Son of God, was sent by the Father to be that new Surety. For Edwards, the entire history of the world is the story of God's plan to glorify himself through the redemption of a people secured by the atoning work of his Son. He believed that "nothing in human history had significance on its own, any more than created nature had a significance on its own. Christ's saving love was the center of all history and defined its meaning."³² This is most fully articulated in his "unfinished masterwork," entitled *A History of the Work of Redemption*, which began as a series of sermons preached in 1739, and was published posthumously by his successors in 1774.

---

29. Ibid., 3:206.
30. Ibid., 3:216.
31. Quoted in Gerstner, *Rational Biblical Theology of Jonathan Edwards*, 2:315.
32. Marsden, *Jonathan Edwards*, 488–89.

From the Fall to the Flood

In this work, Edwards divides the history of redemption into a series of epochs, the first stretching from the fall to the flood. Christ is already present in this period, picking up the pieces as soon as Adam sinned. Edwards writes, "as soon as ever man fell, Christ entered on his Mediatorial work.... He immediately stepped in between a holy, infinite, offended Majesty, and offending mankind,"[33] taking upon himself the offices of prophet, priest, and king. He instantly began to "teach mankind in the exercise of his prophetical office; and also to intercede for fallen man in his priestly office; and he took on him, as it were, the care and burden of the government of the church, and of the world of mankind, from this day forward."[34]

Christ's mediatorial work was necessary because God could have nothing more to do with man post-fall, except through a mediator. Thus, Christ had to commence his work immediately. What this means for Edwards is that everything the Old Testament scriptures say about God's work on man's behalf post-fall should be interpreted christologically, as the New Testament itself seems to do in passages like John 1:18 and Colossians 1:15.[35]

Genesis 3:15 is a passage of particular importance to Edwards, for this text gives us "the first revelation of the covenant of grace" and "the first stone that was laid towards this glorious building, the work of redemption, which will be finished at the end of the world."[36] After this, "the custom of sacrificing was appointed to be a steady type of the sacrifice of Christ until he should come and offer up himself a sacrifice to God."[37] These sacrifices "tended to establish in the minds of God's visible church the necessity of a propitiatory sacrifice in order to the Deity's being satisfied for sin; and so prepares the way for the reception of the glorious gospel that revealed the great sacrifice in the visible church, and not only so, but through the world to mankind."[38] The Anselmian language here is unmistakable, as Edwards frames Christ's atoning work as an act of "satisfaction" for sin. Edwards in

---

33. Edwards, *History of the Work of Redemption*, 21. The work is also available in *Works Online*, vol. 9.
34. Edwards, *History of the Work of Redemption*, 22.
35. Ibid., 23.
36. Ibid., 24–27.
37. Ibid., 26.
38. Ibid., 29.

fact maintains Anselmian language throughout his treatise, providing additional details as his story unfolds, and expanding upon it still further in a series of other writings that will be considered in due course.

Christ's kingly office was first employed when he began gathering his church, which started with the salvation of Adam and Eve, though their son Abel was likely "the first that went to heaven through Christ's redemption . . . and in him the elected angels in heaven had the first opportunity to see so wonderful a thing as the soul of one of the fallen race of mankind, that had been sunk by the Fall into such an abyss of sin and misery, brought to heaven and in the enjoyment of heavenly glory. . . . Thus they, by this, saw the glorious effect of Christ's redemption in the great honour and happiness that was procured for sinful, miserable creatures by it."[39]

As Christ continued building his church during this era, another first occurred: Enoch, who did not die but was directly translated to heaven, was the first to experience "the perfect restoration of the ruins of the Fall with respect to the elect, and restoring man from that destruction that he had brought on himself, in both soul and body. [It was] the first instance that ever was of restoring the ruins of the Fall with respect to the body," providing the whole church with a glimpse of what awaits all the saints.[40]

From the Flood to Abraham

The flood, considered by many to be the supreme Old Testament example of divine judgment, was to Edwards "a work of God that wrought for redemption, since thereby God removed out of the way the enemies and obstacles of it, that were ready to overthrow it." He contends that the violence that ravaged the earth during the pre-flood era was principally violence against the church, seeing that God had declared a state of "enmity" would exist between his people and the Serpent's people from the time of the fall onward. Had God not brought the flood against the enemies of his people, the last of the church would have been wiped from the face of the earth, Edwards argues. Thus, God's destruction of that violent world, and his preservation the church, was an act of *redemption*. It was a fulfillment of his promises in the covenant of grace. Additionally, it was the preservation of the family through which the incarnate Christ would one day come into the world. Moreover, the flood served a typological purpose. As he writes,

39. Ibid., 32–33.
40. Ibid., 39.

That water that washed away the filth of the world, that cleared the world of wicked men, was a type of the blood of Christ, that takes away the sin of the world. That water that delivered Noah and his sons from their enemies is a type of the blood that delivers God's church from their sins, their worst enemies. That water that was so plentiful and abundant that it filled the world, and reached above the tops of the highest mountains, was a type of that blood, the sufficiency of which is so abundant that it is sufficient for the whole world; sufficient to bury the highest mountains of sin.[41]

The judgments God inflicted on the wicked men at the tower of Babel in Genesis 11 likewise contributed to the story of redemption, because that tower was built in opposition to the "great building of God," the church. Had God not destroyed that tower, the enemies of the church might have been able to amass such strength that they could have one day overwhelmed the church of God. Thus, again, God's judgment on the seed of the Serpent was at the same time an act of redemption for the church.[42]

From Abraham to Moses

The call of Abraham marked a significant development in the history of redemption for Edwards, because it marked the first time that God responded to the wickedness of the world by calling a man to *separate* himself from the world, rather than executing a judgment against the world. "This was a new thing," he writes, "a great thing.... This thing was done now about the middle of the space of time between the Fall of man and the coming of Christ." Additionally, "by this call of Abraham, the ancestor of Christ, a foundation was laid for upholding of the church of Christ in the world, until Christ should come."[43]

Abraham also received greater revelations of the covenant of grace than had heretofore been received by the church. It was revealed to him that Christ would come into the world through his line, and that through him all the nations of the earth would be blessed. Additionally, through God's revelation to Abraham, "the great condition of the covenant of grace, which is faith, was now more fully made known."[44]

---

41. Ibid., 46.
42. Ibid., 49–50.
43. Ibid., 54–56.
44. Ibid., 58–59.

There are also some examples of divine judgment during this epoch, such as the destruction of Sodom and Gomorrah. Edwards suggests that God's reason for issuing such devastating judgments in the Old Testament era was because "under the Old Testament there was much more need of some extraordinary, visible, sensible manifestation of God's wrath than in the days of the gospel, since a future state, and the eternal misery of hell, are more clearly revealed, and since the awful justice of God against the sins of men has been so wonderfully displayed in the sufferings of Christ."[45] This statement suggests, as do others in his treatise, that Edwards was a son of the Reformation as well as an Anselmian. Like Anselm, he understood the atonement as an act of satisfaction. And like the Protestant Reformers, he understood that satisfaction to be *penal* in nature; it was an act that satisfied God's "awful justice" against sin. The statement also hints at the way in which Edwards integrated the concepts of God's nature and moral government into a single, coherent system. God judged Sodom and Gomorrah because his holy nature demanded it. At the same time, his judgment was also intended as a public display to vindicate his moral government. For Edwards, the debt of sin has not been fully satisfied until both infractions have been dealt with: the injury to God's person, and the injury to God's position.

From Moses to David

God's decision to deliver the descendants of Abraham from their enslavement in Egypt was "the most remarkable of all the Old Testament redemptions of the church of God and that which was the greatest pledge and forerunner of the future redemption of Christ," Edwards writes. The burning bush, through which Christ spoke to Moses, was also a prophetic representation of his approaching incarnation, death, and resurrection. "It burned but was not consumed; so Christ, though he suffered extremely, yet perished not, but overcame at last, and rose from his sufferings . . . this glorious Redeemer was he that redeemed the church out of Egypt, from under the hand of Pharaoh. He redeemed them, as it is said, from the hard service and cruel drudgery, as Christ redeems his people from the cruel slavery of sin and Satan."[46] The reader may detect echoes of the *Christus Victor* model of the atonement in these words. In doing so, they indicate

---

45. Ibid., 65–66.
46. Ibid., 72.

that Edwards's understanding of the atonement was multidimensional in scope. While Christ's atonement is principally conceived as an act of penal satisfaction in this treatise, Edwards clearly believed that the atonement brought other victories as well, including a spiritual victory over the forces of hell. As Edwards's recounting of the history of redemption continues to unfurl, it will become apparent that his doctrine of atonement contains still more dimensions as well.

Returning to God's rescue of the Israelites from Egypt, Edwards writes that as God did so, he also began forming them into a new nation. To that end he gave them his moral law, which would reveal to them their "sin and misery," to reveal God's "awful and tremendous majesty and justice as a lawgiver," and to "make them sensible of the necessity of Christ as a Savior." It was also given as a "rule of life," to show the church how they should walk before him.[47]

In *Miscellanies* no. 779, Edwards is careful to explain that God's moral law is not an arbitrary set of rules, but an expression of the very nature of God, "an expression of the perfection of the Lawgiver."[48] This helps to further explain the seriousness of human sin. Sin is not merely the violation of a capricious statute, but

> Rebellion against the Lawgiver himself, an opposing the authority of God and a contempt of his infinite majesty. And, it is also an opposition to the holy will of God, so 'tis a contrariety and enmity against the nature of God; for his will [is] but an expression of his holy nature, which is infinitely contrary to sin. . . . And as sin is an opposition to God's nature, so it implies a contrariety to all his perfections, for the nature of God and his perfections are not different; and in being an opposition to his perfections, so it is an opposition to his life and essence and very being, for the being of God and the being of his nature and perfection can't be distinguished. And as sin is an opposition to the nature of God, so 'tis an opposition to his works.[49]

This demonstrates once again Edwards's affinity for Reformation doctrine. Unlike the post-Enlightenment theologians, Edwards perceived an inherent connection between God's law and God's nature; God's moral law is nothing short of a manifestation of himself. To violate this law is therefore

---

47. Ibid., 79–80.
48. Edwards, *Miscellanies* no. 779, in *Works*, 18:443.
49. Edwards, "Christ's Sacrifice an Inducement to His Ministers," in *Works*, 25:663–64.

to rage against the very being of the Lawgiver—an infinitely serious offense. By giving his moral law to the Israelites, God was teaching them these truths. And, he was teaching them about the impossibility of compensating for lawlessness without a qualified mediator. He was teaching them that a sufficient atonement would need to be made, one that would be "equal to the debt," capable of answering the "infinite" demerit of sin.[50]

But beyond the moral law, God also gave the Israelites a "typical law," which included both civil and ceremonial components. These were designed to *surround* the Israelites with types and shadows of the coming Messiah.[51] God also gave his church written scriptures, a land to call their own, and a succession of prophets "whose main business it should be to foreshow Christ and his redemption, and, as his forerunners, prepare the way for his coming."[52]

From David to the Babylonian Captivity

God's anointing of David to be king of Israel "was a great dispensation of God, and a great step taken towards a further advancing of the work of redemption.... David, as he was the ancestor of Christ, so he was the greatest personal type of Christ of all under the Old Testament." His was "the precious seed that virtually contained the Redeemer."[53] David also served the church by composing songs to be sung to the end of the world. These songs focused especially on the coming Redeemer, his "incarnation, life, death, resurrection, ascension into heaven, his satisfaction, intercession; his prophetical, kingly, and priestly office; his glorious benefits in this life and that which is to come; his union with the church, and the blessedness of the church in him; the calling of the Gentiles, the future glory of the church near the end of the world, and Christ's coming to the final judgment."[54]

As great a christological type as David was, however, he still fell far short of the true Messiah, which is why "there had to be a number of typical prophets, priests, and princes to complete one figure or shadow of Christ the antitype, he being the substance of all the types and shadows. Of so

---

50. Edwards, "The Sacrifice of Christ Acceptable," in *Works of Jonathan Edwards*, 14:452.

51. Edwards, *History of the Work of Redemption*, 80.

52. Ibid., 102.

53. Ibid., 104–8.

54. Ibid., 110–11.

much more glory was Christ accounted worthy than Moses, Joshua, David, and Solomon, and all the great prophets, priests, princes, judges, and saviours of the Old Testament put together."[55]

With the coronation of King Solomon and the dedication of the temple, the Old Testament church reached the pinnacle of its glory. From this time until the arrival of Christ, the trajectory of the church would be downward. Edwards suggests a couple of reasons as to why God would have ordained such a downgrade: (1) the declining glory of the law made way for the surpassing glory of the gospel; and (2) the glory of God's power in Christ was made "more conspicuous" by the low state of the church when he came.[56]

From the Babylonian Captivity to the Incarnation of Christ

The period stretching from the Babylonian captivity to the incarnation of Christ marked the final season of preparation for Christ's arrival. During this period great empires rose and fell, as if the world were "in travail to bring forth the Son of God."[57] However, through it all, God preserved his church, purging the church of its idolatry, stripping away those things "wherein consisted the glory of the Jewish dispensation," building anticipation for Christ's arrival, and setting the stage for the worldwide proclamation of the gospel.[58] God raised up Augustus Caesar, ruler of the Roman Empire, to bring peace and stability to the known world, that the gospel might run quickly. "Now all things [were] ready for the birth of Christ. This remarkable universal peace after so many ages of tumult and war was a fit prelude for the ushering of the glorious Prince of Peace into the world."[59]

From Christ's Incarnation to His Resurrection

All that was done from the beginning to the incarnation, from the institution of the covenant of redemption to the historical outworking of the covenant of grace, was building up to the moment when Christ would come

---

55. Ibid., 119.
56. Ibid., 131–32.
57. Ibid., 146–48.
58. Ibid., 160–80.
59. Ibid., 182.

into the world; for it was here, "during the time of Christ's humiliation, from his incarnation to his resurrection, the purchase of redemption was made." The purchase began immediately upon Christ's conception in the womb of the Virgin Mary, and took up the whole of his earthly existence. Nothing was done before the incarnation, and nothing has been done since the resurrection, to pay man's redemption price. It was fully paid during the brief season of Christ's earthly life.[60]

Edwards divides Christ's purchase of redemption into two parts: *satisfaction* and *merit*. Christ's "satisfaction" removed the debt of sin, while his "merit" procured the righteousness which secures the church's eternal rewards. Stated more eloquently, "the satisfaction of Christ is to free us from misery, and the merit of Christ is to purchase happiness for us."[61] Edwards writes that the satisfaction was paid by Christ's sufferings, whereby he "[bore] our punishment in our stead," indicating Edwards's commitment to the Reformation doctrine of *substitutionary* penal satisfaction.[62] The merit, Edwards says, was secured by Christ's life, whereby he answered "the demands of the law."[63]

Though the chief part of Christ's satisfaction was taken up during his passion week, the reality is that his *entire life* was about making satisfaction, Edwards says. "His being born in such a low condition, was to make satisfaction for sin. His being born of a poor virgin, in a stable, and his being laid in a manger; his taking the human nature upon him in its low state, and under those infirmities brought upon it by the Fall; his being born in the form of sinful flesh, had the nature of satisfaction." Likewise, Christ's entire life was taken up in earning merit for men: "His purchase of happiness by his righteousness was also carried on through the whole time of his humiliation until his resurrection; not only in that obedience he performed through the course of his life, but also in the obedience he performed in laying down his life."[64]

---

60. Ibid., 197–98.
61. Ibid., 210.
62. Ibid., 214.
63. Ibid., 212.
64. Ibid., 213.

Christ's Merit Delineated

The righteousness by which Christ earned merit for the church consisted, firstly, of his fulfilling the demands of the covenant of works—that covenant which had been breached by the fall. "That was the covenant that we had broken, and that was the covenant that must be fulfilled." To this end, Christ subjected himself completely to the demands of God's moral law, as well as to the "ceremonial laws" of the Jews and the "mediatorial laws" to which he alone was bound by virtue of his position as Mediator. He perfectly obeyed them all, not only externally, but also with the right inner disposition, despite the manifold trials and temptations he endured. Moreover, he obeyed with "infinite respect to God, and the honour of his law," which was due to his infinite love for God.[65] This point deserves a moment of reflection. Edwards states that Christ came to "honor" God's law, which sounds something like what the proponents of the so-called governmental theory of the atonement were saying. However, it is also worth noting that Edwards does not make this statement *at the expense* of the doctrine of substitutionary penal satisfaction, as did the proponents of the governmental theory. This seems to be the key difference between the views of Edwards and Grotius. Edwards presents sin as opposition to God's nature and moral government; thus, the atonement must *both* propitiate God's wrath and honor his authority. While Grotius accepted the latter point, he rejected the former.

Christ's righteous acts also encompassed "the different parts of his life wherein they were performed," Edwards says. Christ was perfectly obedient in his private life, as well as his public life; in childhood, as well as in adulthood.[66] Moreover, his righteousness encompassed those *virtues* that

---

65. Ibid., 216–20. Early in his ministerial career, Edwards suggested a modified understanding of the covenants of grace and works, arguing that they were in fact the same covenant, differing only in the sense that they had different federal heads. As he writes in *Miscellanies* no. 30, "With reference to what has been before spoken of the covenant [no. 2]. Covenant is taken very variously in Scripture, sometimes for a divine promise, sometimes for a divine promise on conditions. But if we speak of the covenant God has made with man stating the condition of eternal life, God never made but one with man to wit, the covenant of works; which never yet was abrogated, but is a covenant stands in full force to all eternity without the failing of one tittle. The covenant of grace is not another covenant made with man upon the abrogation of this, but a covenant made with Christ to fulfill it. And for this end came Christ into the world, to fulfill the law, or covenant of works, for all that receive him." In *Works*, 18:217.

66. Edwards, *History of the Work of Redemption*, 220.

he exercised throughout his life, including his "holy fear and reverence" of God, his "humility, patience, and contempt for the world," and his "meekness and love" toward men.[67] As stated earlier, Christ's righteousness was both external and internal.

Christ's Satisfaction Delineated

Christ's work of making satisfaction for sin began with the "uncommon humiliation and sufferings" of his infancy, which included his birth in a manger, his subjection to persecution by Herod, and all that added to his trials in youth. It included his "private life at Nazareth," where he labored in obscurity for so many years. It included the humiliations of his public life, from his poverty, to the "hatred and reproach" he experienced, to the "buffetings of Satan" he endured, to his passion, "by which principally he made satisfaction to the justice of God for the sins of men."[68]

The entirety of Christ's earthly life, then, from conception to death, was taken up in that great work of making satisfaction for sin. As he breathed his last upon the cross, declaring "It is finished,"

> Thus was finished the greatest and most wonderful thing that ever was done. Now the angels beheld the most wonderful sight they ever saw. Now was accomplished the main thing that had been pointed at by the various institutions of the ceremonial law, and by all the typical dispensations, and by all the sacrifices from the beginning of the world . . . then was finished the great work, the purchase of our redemption, for which such great preparation had been made from the beginning of the world. Then was finished all that was required in order to satisfy the threatenings of the law, and all that was necessary in order to satisfy divine justice; then the utmost that vindicating justice demanded, even the whole debt, was paid. Then was finished the whole of the purchase of eternal life. And now there is no need of any thing more to be done towards a purchase of salvation for sinners; nor has ever any thing been done since, nor will any thing more be done for ever and ever.[69]

---

67. Ibid., 226–29.
68. Ibid., 231–34.
69. Ibid., 238–39.

CONCLUSION

Coming to the end of our study of Edwards's basic theological framework, it is apparent that Edwards possessed a far greater affinity for traditional Reformed orthodoxy than he did for post-Enlightenment theology. He posited a God who is infinitely glorious in all his perfections, who is defined by love, and who finds supreme delight in communicating his perfections to intelligent creatures that they might bask in those perfections with him. He defines God's moral law as the ethical expression of his own nature, and not as an arbitrary apparatus. He teaches that Adam was created in righteousness, but fell into sin of his own volition. He defines sin as the violation of God's law and the despising of God's nature—crimes that incur a legal penalty. And, while emphasizing a number of aspects of Christ's atonement, he is also careful to explain the atonement as an act of substitutionary penal satisfaction.

The only feature that really sets Edwards apart from his Reformed orthodox predecessors seems to be his predilection for trying to "solve the unsolvable," [70] often refusing to accept that theological challenges are incapable of being resolved. This is evident, for example, in his attempts to understand the nature of the Trinity and in his efforts to explain how Adam, created in righteousness, could have given himself over to sin. His proposed solutions sometimes leave traditional Reformed thinkers scratching their heads, but his musings in no way threaten the basic framework of traditional Reformed orthodoxy, which he held. These musings simply reveal a mind that refused to accept defeat, as well as one that stuck to its commitments. Edwards's eleventh resolution, written when he was just nineteen years old, says, "Resolved, when I think of any theorem in divinity to be solved, immediately to do what I can towards solving it."[71]

---

70. Gerstner, *Jonathan Edwards*, 40.
71. Edwards, *Resolutions* no. 11, in *Works*, 16:754.

Chapter 6

The Vital Content of Edwards's Doctrine of Atonement

THE BASIC FRAMEWORK OF Edwards's doctrine of atonement follows the same general contours as that of his Reformed orthodox predecessors. In those areas where there is divergence, it is more often in style rather than substance. He shares the Reformed orthodox view that God's law is an extension of his nature, that sin is the violation of God's law and the rejection of his authority, and that the atonement was an act of substitutionary satisfaction. Like them, he also emphasizes the threefold office of Christ as prophet, priest, and king, subsuming Christ's satisfaction for sin under his role as priest. And, like the Puritans, he approaches the atonement from a covenantal perspective, placing Christ's atonement in the larger context of the covenants of redemption, works, and grace. In this chapter, we move from the framework of Edwards's theory to its vital content, examining more closely Edwards's perspective on such matters as the necessity, value, nature, extent, and application of the atonement. Our discoveries here should provide a more definitive answer to the question at the heart of our study.

THE NECESSITY OF CHRIST'S ATONEMENT

John Gerstner contends that "everything Edwards says about the sacrifice and the satisfaction of Christ implies its absolute necessity."[1] While this

---

1. Gerstner, *Rational Biblical Theology of Jonathan Edwards*, 2:429.

may be a bit hyperbolic, the general idea is surely correct. Throughout his surviving works Edwards declares, both explicitly and implicitly, that the atoning work of Christ was the only conceivable means by which sinful men could have been reconciled to a sinless God. Edwards bases this point on two grounds: (1) sin has irrevocable consequences; and (2) Christ is uniquely qualified to bear the full weight of those consequences for man.

The Irrevocable Consequences of Sin

In *Miscellanies* no. 779, Edwards offers five reasons as to why God must punish sin. First, he says, "justice requires that sins be punished, because sin deserves punishment." Sin deserves an infinite punishment, in fact, because sin in an infinite evil, being against the infinitely glorious God. Secondly, God's holiness requires infinite punishment for sins, because holiness is by definition indignant toward sin. Since God will forever be holy, his outrage at sin will never cease. Thirdly, God must punish sin because if he did not his position as moral governor of the world would fall into contempt. Edwards explains:

> God is to be considered in this affair not merely as the governor of the world of creatures, to order things between one creature and another, but as the supreme regulator or Rector of the universality of things, the orderer of things relating to the whole compass of existence, including himself, to maintain the rights of the whole, and decorum through the whole, and to maintain his own rights, and the due honor of his own perfections, as well as to keep justice among creatures. 'Tis fit that there should be one that has this office, and the office properly belongs to the supreme being. And if he should fail of doing justice to him[self] in a needed vindication of his own majesty and glory, it would be an immensely greater failure of his rectoral justice than if he should deprive the creatures, that are beings of infinitely less consequence, of their rights.

Edwards is saying that God's position as moral governor includes two responsibilities: he must maintain with zeal the honor of his own glory, and he must "keep justice" among his creatures. If God did not punish sin, his own rights as God would be trampled underfoot and lawlessness would completely overtake the world. God could not permit this.

Fourthly, Edwards argues that God must punish sin in order to maintain the authority of his law. When the threatenings of a law are not enforced, he writes, "in such proportion does the law lose its strength, and fails of the proper nature and power of a law, [it] degenerates toward the nature of request, and expression of will or desire to receive love or respect." Edwards also adds that the law was established for the common good, which means that if the sanctions of the law are not upheld, everyone will suffer in the end. Therefore, "tis not only unfit that [the law] should give place to rebellion, as this would be a dishonor to the excellency of the law and Lawgiver, but also a wrong to the public good, which the supreme Rector of the world has the care of and is the guardian of." He continues: "If the rule [i.e. the law] be perfect, perfectly right and just and holy, and with infinite wisdom adapted to the good of the whole, then the public good require that it be strongly established." And again, "everything by which it is weakened, is a damage and loss to the commonwealth of being."

Fifthly, God must punish sin because his truthfulness is at stake. When God threatened punishment for sin in the garden of Eden, he was giving both a prophecy and a promise. If he did not repay sin with judgment in the end, he would be guilty of uttering false prophecy.[2] This point is made in greater detail in *Miscellanies* no. 915:

> Had God violated his word (in the threatening of death for sin), he had justified the devil in his argument for man's rebellion. The devil's argument is a plain contradiction to God's threatening. God affirms the certainty of death, the devil affirms the certainty of life. . . . Had no punishment been inflicted, the devil had not been a liar from the beginning (John 8:44). God would have honored the tempter, and justified the charge he brought against him, and owned that envy the devil accused him of, and thereby have rendered the devil the fittest object for love and trust. As the devil charged God with a lie, so had no punishment been inflicted, God would have condemned himself, and declared Satan instead of a lying tempter to be the truest counselor. He had exposed himself to contempt, and advanced the credit of his enemy, and so set up the devil as God instead of himself. It concerned God therefore to manifest himself true, and the devil a liar; and acquaint the world, that not himself, but the evil spirit, was their deceiver, and that he meant as he spake.[3]

---

2. Edwards, *Miscellanies* no. 779, in *Works*, 18:434–49.

3. Edwards, *Miscellanies* no. 915, in *Works*, 20:165. Edwards is citing Stephen Charnock here.

In summary, Edwards believed that Christ's atonement was necessary because God's threatened punishment against sin could not be revoked. Sin is an infinite evil deserving infinite punishment; if God refused to punish sin, he would not be righteous. Moreover, he would be a dishonorable governor, having no concern for his own rights or the common good. He would be utterly despising his own just laws, and would be declaring himself a liar and the devil a truth-teller, in effect "setting up the devil as God instead of himself." God therefore *had* to punish sin.

The Uniqueness of Christ to Pay Sin's Price

An atonement was necessary for men's salvation because God simply cannot ignore the offense of sin. But why did *Christ* have provide that atonement? Edwards believed that Christ was necessary because Christ alone was capable of paying sin's infinite penalty. Only his blood would do. Edwards explains why in his sermon on Hebrews 9:12: "There are no others but Jesus Christ alone, in heaven or in earth, that has any power to exercise in any of the functions of Christ's priesthood. There is none that can offer any satisfaction but he alone, neither is their salvation in any other. . . . There is no other blood but this precious blood that will cleanse us, no other sacrifice but this Lamb of God, this spotless, unblemished Lamb who was blameless and perfectly innocent, perfectly holy, perfectly—yea, infinitely—amiable and lovely."[4]

Edwards expands upon this idea in his sermon on Hebrews 9:13–14, preached in 1738. He explains that Christ is the only "God-man"; therefore, only he is capable of representing the interests of both parties, and only he could offer a blood atonement that was both human and all-sufficient.[5]

In his sermon from Luke 22:44, delivered to his Northampton congregation in 1739, he continued to stress the necessity of Christ's intervention: "Christ would not undergo these sufferings needlessly, if sinners could be saved without. If there was not an absolute necessity of his suffering them in order to their salvation, he desired that the cup might pass from him. But if sinners, on whom he had set his love, could not agreeably to the will of God, be saved without his drinking it, he chose that the will of God should be done."[6] Thus, Christ's blood atonement was both an inherent necessity

---

4. Edwards, "Christ's Sacrifice," in *Works*, 10:594–604.
5. Edwards, sermon no. 495, in *Works Online*, vol. 53.
6. Edwards, "Christ's Agony," cited in Gerstner, *Rational Biblical Theology of Jonathan*

and a necessity by virtue of divine decree. No one but the incarnate Christ was qualified to make proper atonement, and God had decreed no other way for men to be saved.

In summary, Edwards mounts a variety of arguments to establish the necessity of Christ's atoning work. He explains that sin, being a crime of infinite proportions, requires a penalty that finite man can never fully pay; that the divine law, if it is to be regarded as law, must have its punishments inflicted; that God, being just and holy, must judge that which deserves judgement; that, as a good moral governor, he must maintain his own rights and the good of his subjects; and that, as a truthful being, he must carry out his threats. And, since Christ alone is the God-man, infinitely holy and perfectly human, he alone was qualified to stand between God and the sinner, to pay the infinite penalty that was due, and to facilitate man's reconciliation with God.

THE VALUE OF CHRIST'S ATONEMENT

Closely related to the question of necessity is the question of value. Here, Edwards is crystal clear: because Christ was the God-man, his blood was of infinite worth—fully sufficient to pay the infinite penalty incurred by man's sin. As he declares in his sermon from Hebrews 9:12,

> All created beings are nothing worth to God in comparison of the least drop of Christ's blood. The blood of Christ is united to the Godhead personally: it is the blood of God, and is so-called in Scripture. Acts 20:28, "Take heed to feed the church of God, which he hath purchased with his own blood." Wherefore, it must needs be a most precious thing; it must be of infinite worth and value, and therefore sufficient to purge away sin which is of infinite demerit. The least drop of Christ's blood is of more worth in God's accounts than all the sacrifices that ever were slain from the beginning of the world till that time.[7]

He makes a similar claim in his sermon on Hebrews 9:13–14, saying, "it was the deity of Christ that gave that infinite value and virtue to his sufferings. This altar [i.e., the altar of his deity] so sanctifies the gift that it renders the blood of Christ infinitely precious so that it is called the blood

---

Edwards, 2:446.

7. Edwards, "Christ's Sacrifice," in *Works*, 10:599.

The Vital Content of Edwards's Doctrine of Atonement

of God (Acts 20:28). The union of the gift with this altar made it infinitely valuable."[8]

This theme is repeated in his *Miscellanies*. In entry no. 447 he writes, "by reason of the infinite dignity of his person, his sufferings were looked upon [as] of infinite value, and equivalent to the eternal sufferings of a finite creature. And he spilled his blood from respect to the glory of God's majesty that we had injured, and from respect to God's will commanding him: his obedience was of infinite value, because he was at infinite expense to obey."[9] And in no. 483, "because of the infinite worthiness and excellency of Christ and his dearness to the Father, the Father is willing for his sake to accept of those that have deserved infinite ill at his hands."[10]

Edwards rejected the notion, promulgated by men like Socinus, that Christ's death could at best pay just one man's debt. He also rejected the notion, popularized by Grotius, that God's acceptance of Christ's sacrifice entailed a "relaxing" of the law. On the contrary, Edwards believed Christ's deity guaranteed that his singular sacrifice was sufficient for the sins of the whole world. In fact, like the Reformed orthodox before him, Edwards used the phrase "fully equivalent" to describe the relationship between what man owed and what Christ endured.[11] Christ, as the God-man, was able to provide an infinitely valuable atonement. He was "big enough" for the task.[12]

Beyond all of this, Edwards offered seven additional arguments supporting his contention that Christ's atonement was all-sufficient. First, Christ's sacrifice was the only requirement stipulated in the covenant of redemption. If more was necessary to deal with sin, more would have been required. Second, Christ's atonement was the basis upon which Old Testament saints received their salvation. Third, Christ's atonement was the fulfillment of all the typological sacrifices of the Old Testament. Fourth, its sufficiency is evidenced by the fact that God has not appointed any priests since Christ. Fifth, Christ's sacrifice was offered only once, suggesting that

---

8. Edwards, sermon no. 495, in *Works Online*, vol. 53. For the sake of clarity, I have converted Edwards's shorthand into standard English.

9. Edwards, *Miscellanies* no. 447, in *Works*, 13:495.

10. Edwards, *Miscellanies* no. 483, in *Works*, 13:524–27.

11. Edwards, sermon on Luke 22:44, cited in Gerstner, *Rational Biblical Theology of Jonathan Edwards*, 2:453. Edwards affirms the same in his sermons on Isaiah 53:3 and Galatians 2:17.

12. Edwards, *History of the Work of Redemption*, in *Works*, 19:335. Another reference to the infinite value of Christ's atonement can be found in *Religious Affections*, in *Works*, 2:302.

it was fully sufficient the first time. Sixth, Christ's subsequent exaltation, combined with the subsequent outpouring of the Spirit, indicate that it was all-sufficient. Seventh, Edwards argued that the great success of the Great Awakening testified to its all-sufficiency for saving men.[13]

THE NATURE OF CHRIST'S ATONEMENT

Our study of Edwards's basic framework revealed a multifaceted perspective on the nature of Christ's work, with a clear emphasis on the concepts of satisfaction and penal substitution. The following paragraphs will provide a more detailed explanation of these concepts from Edwards's perspective, as well as reveal some additional facets not yet closely observed.

The Atonement as Substitutionary Penal Satisfaction

The concept of Christ's atonement as penal satisfaction was at the very center of Edwards's doctrinal system. He says as much in his *Controversies* notebook: "The importance of all Christian doctrines whatsoever, will naturally be denied in consequence of denying that one great doctrine of the necessity of Christ's satisfaction to divine justice. . . . This is as it were the center and hinge of all doctrines of pure revelation."[14]

The words "sacrifice" and "satisfaction" appear more than any other terms in the Edwards corpus to describe the nature of Christ's atonement, Edwards often using the terms interchangeably—and this makes sense. Christ's death cannot be called a "sacrifice" unless it was designed to accomplish some specific good for man. All men die, after all, but not all men's deaths are sacrificial. For Edwards, Christ's death was a sacrifice *because* it was offered as a penal satisfaction for sinners. This is evident throughout his extant works. In his sermon on Revelation 5:12, preached in 1731–32, he writes, "Christ's death did not merely satisfy for sin. Christ's death was a sacrifice to satisfy divine justice for our sins."[15] Likewise, in his sermon on Psalm 110:4, preached in 1744, he maintains that Christ's sacrifice had two primary functions: (1) "Removing God's anger by satisfaction

---

13. Edwards, sermon no. 495, in *Works Online*, vol. 53.
14. Edwards, *Controversies*, in *Works Online*, vol. 27.
15. Edwards, sermon no. 263, in *Works Online*, vol. 47.

to God's justice"; and (2) "Procuring the favour of God and the fruits by his merits."[16] In his sermon on Galatians 2:20, he declares that Christ satisfies God's wrath and lifts the curse of the law,[17] and in his sermon on Hebrews 12:2, he connects the concepts of sacrifice and satisfaction again: "Jesus Christ has satisfied divine justice; he offered up that that fully satisfied infinite justice. Our glorious Savior descended to the earth and here made a sacrifice of himself that justice might be satisfied. In order to satisfy, it was requisite that he should bear that which justice required. Now justice requires the greatest pain and horror in the soul; this Christ underwent, etc."[18] In his sermon on Ephesians 5:27–27, he refers specifically to God's *vindicative* justice as the reason for Christ's atonement. He declares that the church was "fast bound under [divine justice] and could not deliver herself," so Christ offered himself to pay her ransom: "He gave himself to the revenging justice of God. . . . He gave himself up to divine wrath." He was "wholly in body and soul to be as it were consumed by the justice and wrath of God . . . to be all a sacrifice to justice and divine wrath."[19]

Edwards was also careful to stress that Christ's penal satisfaction for sin was a *substitutionary* penal satisfaction. In his sermon on Hebrews 9:13–14, he writes that Christ suffered "in the stead" of sinful men; that he "represented him that sinned."[20] This substitution, Edwards argues, was accomplished by means of a legal exchange. Commenting on 1 Corinthians 5:21, he writes, "'He was made sin,' i.e. sin was imputed to him. And what sin was it? Why, that sin that was *in us*. So we are made 'the righteousness of God.' But what righteousness of God is it that we are made? Why, that which was in Christ our Mediator."[21] In his *Controversies* notebook, he writes that Christ "imput[ed] his sufferings to the sinner as one that in that manner stood for the sinner and was his representative."[22] In another section of his *Controversies* notebook he writes, "God's saints in Israel supposed that the Messiah, when he came . . . would make an end of their sins and wholly abolish the guilt of them by an atonement which he should

---

16. Edwards, sermon no. 746, in *Works Online*, vol. 67.
17. Edwards, sermon no. 091, in *Works Online*, vol. 43.
18. Edwards, "Christ's Sacrifice," in *Works*, 10:598.
19. Edwards, sermon no. 358, in *Works Online*, vol. 50. The sermon also remains to be edited.
20. Edwards, sermon no. 495, in *Works Online*, vol. 53.
21. Edwards, *Notes on Scripture* no. 318, in *Works*, 15:296.
22. Edwards, *Controversies*, in *Works Online*, vol. 27.

make; and that the guilt of their sins, though removed from them and as it were laid upon that divine person who dwelt on the propitiatory in the temple, and was by him taken on himself, yet would not properly be abolished and made an end of till he should come."[23] And in *Miscellanies* no. 846, he writes, "Indeed, how far the dignity or worthiness of Christ's person comes into consideration in determining the propriety of his being accepted as a representative of sinners."[24] Perhaps the clearest statement of all is found in *Miscellanies* no. 1035: "Christ indeed suffered the full punishment of the sin that was imputed to him, or offered that to God that was fully and completely equivalent to what we owed to divine justice for our sins." The sin for which Christ was punished was not "sin that he himself committed, but that sin that was laid upon him, or that he took upon him."[25]

For Edwards, as for Ames and so many others in the Reformed tradition, penal substitution was rooted in the broader context of his federalist theology. As he explains in his famous discourse, "Justification by Faith Alone,"

> Adam was not to have the reward [of eternal life] merely on account of his being innocent; if so, [God] would have had it fixed upon him at once, as soon as ever he was created . . . but he was to have the reward on account of his activeness in obedience . . .
> Christ is our second federal head, and is called the second Adam . . . because he acted the part for us, that the first Adam should have done: when he had undertaken to stand in our stead, he was looked upon, and treated as though he were guilty with our guilt; and by his satisfying, or bearing the penalty, he did as it were free himself from this guilt. But by this, the second Adam did only bring himself into the state that the first Adam was in on the first moment of his existence, viz. a state of mere freedom from guilt; and hereby indeed was free from any obligation to suffer punishment: but this being supposed, there was need of something further, even a positive obedience, in order to his obtaining, as our second Adam, the reward of eternal life.[26]

Edwards's commitment to the atonement as an act of substitutionary penal satisfaction is even evident in his evangelistic appeals. One example

---

23. Edwards, *Controversies*, "Justification," in *Works Online*, vol. 27.
24. Edwards, *Miscellanies* no. 846, in *Works*, 20:67.
25. Edwards, *Miscellanies* no. 1035, in *Works*, 20:375–76.
26. Edwards, *Justification by Faith Alone*, in *Works*, 19:187.

The Vital Content of Edwards's Doctrine of Atonement

will suffice, this one from his sermon entitled "The Justice of God in the Damnation of Sinners," preached around 1735, and based on Romans 3:19:

> Christ came into the world on this errand, to offer himself as an atonement, to answer for our desert of punishment. But how is it possible that you should be willing to accept Christ, as an atonement for that guilt that you be not sensible that you have? How can you be willing to have Christ for a Savior from a desert of hell, if you be not sensible that you have a desert of hell? If you have not really deserved everlasting burnings in hell, then the very offer of an atonement for such a desert is an imposition upon you. If you have no such guilt upon you, then the very offer of a satisfaction for that guilt is an injury, but it implies that in it a charge of guilt that you are free from. . . . A man that is not convinced that he has deserved so dreadful a punishment, can't willingly submit to be charged with it; if he thinks he is willing, it is but a mere forced, feigned business; because in his heart he looks upon himself greatly injured: and therefore he can't freely accept of Christ, under that notion, of a Savior from that guilt, and from the desert of such a punishment.[27]

On the question of why God could not reconcile with repentant sinners without penal satisfaction, Edwards answers that even the best repentance is "as little as none in comparison to the greatness of the injury." Indeed, it would be as dishonorable for God to accept man's repentance without satisfaction, as it would be for him to reconcile with a man who had offered no repentance at all, for the two are hardly different. This gets us to Edwards's definition of true repentance. Repentance is not satisfaction, Edwards says. It is rather a rejection of one's sins and a trusting in the satisfaction that was made by Christ.[28]

Regarding the question of how the punishment inflicted on the sinless Christ could satisfy the demands of the law against sinners, Edwards returns to the theme of divine love. He argues that Christ's love for the sinner has the effect of "thoroughly assuming them into union with himself," which is only possible with an infinite love such as Christ possessed—a love that "is sufficient to cause the lover to place himself in the beloved's stead for his sake in the most extreme case, and even in the case of [the] beloved's loss of his all, and his utter destruction."[29] Such a love, Edwards says, is

---

27. Edwards, "The Justice of God in the Damnation of Sinners," in *Works*, 19:362.
28. Edwards, *Miscellanies* no. 00, in *Works*, 13:188.
29. The same point is made in his sermon entitled "The Sacrifice of Christ Acceptable."

sufficient to unite two parties together so that they may be considered as one, for in such an instance the lover's affection has caused him to set a value upon the beloved's welfare that is equal to the value he has placed on his own.[30] In *Miscellanies* no. *b*, Edwards draws an analogy from the human body. He explains that if a man steals with his hands, justice does not require that the hands themselves receive the punishment for the offense. So long as the man himself is punished, justice is satisfied. And so it is with Christ. Sinful men committed the offense, but the union formed by Christ's love for his people means that justice may be satisfied by his punishment, even though he did not technically commit the offense.[31] The union "holds" with God, Edwards says.[32]

In answer to the objection that it would be unseemly for a perfect being like Christ to unite himself in love to sinners, Edwards argues that it would only be problematic if Christ was unwilling to "bear their guilt himself and suffer their punishment." But by acknowledging the "infinite evil and ill desert" of their sin, and by "appearing ready to suffer the punishment deserved himself," to "receive the Father's wrath to them" himself, Christ was able to unite himself in love to the sinner without becoming a partaker in their sins.[33]

Another question near the center of the atonement debate concerns the degree of equivalence between Christ's sufferings and that deserved by sinners. In other words, did Christ suffer exactly the same punishment that sinners deserved? The Reformed orthodox answered this question in the affirmative, while the Grotians and Rationalists answered in the negative. Earlier, we saw that Edwards answered in the affirmative. However, in his *Miscellanies* we discover that Edwards's full answer was actually a bit more nuanced than he let on in some of his sermons. In *Miscellanies* no. 321b, for example, he writes that Christ "suffered the very same misery that sinners are condemned to, *so far as a person of his nature was capable of.*" In what ways was Christ incapable of suffering the same misery as the damned? Edwards argues that Christ knew, even on the cross, that God was "not

---

Edwards writes, "He laid down his life out of love to us; he has been pleased to unite himself to us in his heart, to love us so as to put himself in our stead in the most extreme case." In *Works*, 14:453.

30. Edwards, *Miscellanies* no. 483, in *Works*, 13:524–27.
31. Edwards, *Miscellanies* no. *b*, in *Works*, 13:164–65.
32. Edwards, *Miscellanies* no. 398, in *Works*, 13:463–64.
33. Edwards, *Miscellanies* no. 483, in *Works*, 13:524–27.

really angry with him." Moreover, Christ knew that his sufferings would not last forever.[34] These statements suggest that Edwards did not question the equivalence of Christ's sufferings in any real sense, but only in a psychological sense. In other words, he questioned the premise that Christ's mental and emotional state could have been identical with the damned in hell during his passion, because he was the God-man; and in experience, he was absolutely holy. And in saying that "God was not really angry" with Christ, Edwards was simply affirming that the sin Christ bore was an imputed sin, since Christ in his character was completely holy. Nothing more should be made of it than that.

Edwards continued thinking about Christ's psychological state on the cross for some time. *Miscellanies* no. 366 reveals another turn in his thinking. The entry reads, "Christ's suffering was *far less* than the sufferings of the damned, upon several other accounts besides his not having despair. He had at the same time a sense of the glory of God . . ." Edwards never finished this sentence, however, and at some later point he even crossed the entire entry out with a great X,[35] suggesting that he was uncomfortable with his own wording here. And by entry no. 516 he was even reversing course. He again writes that Christ's experience of suffering could not have been exactly like that of the damned, but this time he argues that Christ's experience was "much *more* grievous" than that of the damned. This is because, unlike the damned, Christ had a full comprehension of "the worth of the good that he lost," the "good" being the love and happiness of the Father.[36] And by *Miscellanies* no. 781 he returned to standard Reformed orthodoxy, leaving behind his speculations about Christ's psychological state, writing only that Christ's suffering was "fully proportionable to the hatefulness of the crime [of human sin]."[37]

Edwards's final discussion of this subject occurs in *Miscellanies* no. 1005, written in the early 1740s. As such, it should probably be regarded as his most mature thinking on the subject. Here, he returns to the matter of Christ's psychological state. He repeats his assertion from a previous entry, saying that "Christ suffered the wrath of God for men's sins *in such a way as he was capable of.*" This time, his explanation is the following: Christ, unlike

---

34. Edwards, *Miscellanies* no. 321b, in *Works*, 13:402. Italics added.

35. Edwards, *Miscellanies* no. 366, in *Works*, 13:437. Italics added. Information provided in the footnote by the editor.

36. Edwards, *Miscellanies* no. 516, in *Works*, 18:62. Italics added.

37. Edwards, *Miscellanies* no. 716, in *Works*, 18:347.

those in hell, "knew that God was not angry with him personally, knew that God did not hate him, but infinitely loved him." Therefore, the wrath that Christ experienced on the cross was the experience of (1) having a full sense of God's disposition toward sin, and (2) having a full sense of what sin deserves. He was given a full sense of the "hatefulness" of sin, without any "pleasant or sweet idea" to reduce that sense. Edwards summarizes: "If Christ had had a perfectly clear and full idea of what the damned suffer in hell, the suffering he would have had in the mere presence of that idea would have been perfectly equal to the thing itself."[38] Thus, for Edwards, the full *idea* of something is equal to the *reality* of it; and it is in this sense that we may declare Christ's sufferings were equivalent to the sufferings of the damned. The punishment he endured for sin was qualitatively equal to what sinner's deserve, though, due to his unique nature and the fact that his sins were imputed, not inherent, his *experience* of the suffering was unique.

Edwards continued this entry by musing still further about the psychology of Christ as he lay suspended on the cross, this time turning his attention to Christ's love. Edwards writes, "Christ's love then brought his elect infinitely near to him, in that great act and suffering wherein he especially stood for them, and was substituted in their stead; and his love and pity fixed the idea of them in his mind, as if he had really been they, and fixed their calamity in his mind, as though it really was his." He then offers a commentary on his own words: "a very strong and lively love and pity towards the miserable tends to make their case our own . . . it doth in our idea place us in their stead under their misery with a most lively feeling sense of that misery, as it were feeling it for them, actually suffering it in their stead by strong sympathy."[39]

The repetition of phrases like "as he was capable of," "as it were," etc., combined with the idea of Christ's sufferings as an extreme example of empathy, have led some, like Edwards Amasa Park, to suggest that Edwards's views had much more in common with the Grotian theory than the penal substitution theory. However, this would seem to be an unwarranted conclusion. As J. I. Packer explains, the penal substitution theory of the atonement is merely "a model setting forth the meaning of the atonement." It is *not* a system purporting to explain all the mechanics of the atonement. As such, the theory leaves unexplored a number of the atonement's deeper

---

38. Edwards, *Miscellanies* no. 1005, in *Works*, 20:329–34.
39. Ibid., 20:332.

mysteries, such as how Christ could be "made sin" for the elect, or exactly how the union of Christ and his elect was achieved.[40]

Taking Edwards's work on the whole, it is clear that all of the essential pieces of the penal substitutionary model are there. He affirms that humanity's sin deserves God's retributive justice, and that men cannot remedy this problem themselves. He affirms that Christ endured men's sins in their stead, accepting the just judgments of God on the sinners' behalf. And, he affirms that Christ's work is the sole basis upon which men can be reconciled to God. In light of this, we conclude that all Edwards was doing in these *Miscellanies* entries was seeking to probe the mysteries of the *mechanics* of Christ's atonement. His words do not undermine the model of penal substitution, but merely try to explain some of the details left unexplained by it. It is for the student of Edwards to decide whether his musings have merit. What cannot be doubted, however, is Edwards's commitment to the penal substitutionary view.

The Atonement as Non-Substitutionary Satisfaction

The doctrine of substitutionary penal satisfaction was at the heart of Edwards's understanding of the atonement. Even so, this doctrine does not represent his total understanding of the atonement. As the following paragraphs demonstrate, Edwards believed that Christ's death also served as a penal example, publicly vindicating God's honor and law, which God also required before sin's penalty could be fully satisfied.

In *Miscellanies* no. 161, for example, Edwards writes, "God gave a law, that [Adam] might have an opportunity to honor God by obeying it; and God now insists upon satisfaction, that this law may not go without its honor. And it's certain, that Christ by his obedience has done much more honor to God's law than Adam by his obedience could have done, and God is hereby satisfied."[41] It is important to notice that Edwards speaks of honoring *God* and honoring the *law* as if they were synonymous ideas. This is likely owing to the fact that Edwards saw the law as the outward expression of God's nature and position. Therefore, to honor the law is to honor God, and to honor God is to honor his law. By rendering perfect obedience to the law, Edwards maintained that Christ honored the law, which is to say that he showed proper respect to both the person and position of God—some-

---

40. Packer, "What Did the Cross Achieve?," 24–33.
41. Edwards, *Miscellanies* no. 161, in *Works*, 13:311.

thing the first Adam failed to do. As a result, God was *satisfied*, Edwards said, meaning that Christ's obedience fully answered God's demand that his glory and government be given the public respect that they are due.

In *Miscellanies* no. 451, written around 1730, Edwards continued this thought by writing, "the sacrifice of [Christ] may properly be said to be infinitely holy, as it was an expression of an infinite regard to the holiness, majesty, etc. of God."[42] And, in *Miscellanies* no. 452 he again stated that Christ's death showed "infinite respect" to God, demonstrating that "he was willing to be at infinite expense, rather than the salvation of men should be any injury to the glory of God's majesty" and that "he was at infinite expense to obey God's commands to him."[43] The idea here is that God required a public vindication of his authority for the penalty of sin to be satisfied, and Christ was more than willing to give that honor to God.

Several years later, in his sermon on John 10:18, Edwards would emphasize the idea again: "Christ . . . showed his infinite esteem of God . . . in that when he had a mind that sinners should be freed, he had rather bear such great suffering, and be so exceedingly humbled, than that their salvation should be to his dishonor."[44] Similar language appeared again in a 1736 sermon on Revelation 14:13, where he declared that Christ's death "was a testimony of God's abhorrence sufficient for the greatest wickedness that ever was in the world that Christ the eternal Son died for it."[45] Thus, two concepts came together for Edwards here: sin injured God's honor, meaning that God required Christ's atonement to include a public vindication of that honor for sins to be satisfied; and, Christ's regard for the Father was so great that he *wanted* God's honor to receive a public vindication.

This was in fact a recurrent theme in Edwards's writings. Returning to his sermon on John 10:18, Edwards also declared, "Christ by his death in a transcendent manner glorified the authority of God, as it was to atone for the injury and offense done to God's authority by men's sins. Christ hereby gave his testimony that so sacred was the divine authority, that nothing less than his own blood would atone for the contempt of it."[46] And in *Miscel-*

---

42. Edwards, *Miscellanies* no. 451, in *Works*, 13:498.

43. Edwards, *Miscellanies* no. 452, in *Works*, 13:498.

44. Edwards, "The Free and Voluntary Suffering and Death of Christ," in *Works*, 19:504.

45. Cited in Gerstner, *Rational Biblical Theology of Jonathan Edwards*, 2:436.

46. Edwards, "The Free and Voluntary Suffering and Death of Christ," in *Works*, 19:503.

lanies no. 483 he wrote, "it was judged meet that Christ himself should do that honor to God's authority . . . by perfectly obeying his law, that he might do that honor to God's authority by his obedience, the principle instance of which was his laying down his life in obedience to his Father. Christ having obeyed and given this honor and respect to God's authority, it is given for us."[47] And in *Miscellanies* no. 1146 he wrote that the *goal* of Christ's sufferings was "his openly honoring God by such a manifestation of his love."[48]

Harmonizing the Concepts of Penal Substitution and Penal Example in Edwards's Doctrine of Atonement

Edwards's doctrine of atonement, then, included two prominent concepts: Christ as a penal substitute, and Christ as a penal example. As the two concepts are placed side by side, it becomes apparent that these ideas were not contradictory in Edwards's mind, but complementary. Indeed, as we consider these concepts in light of Edwards's complete theological system, we discover that the harmony and symmetry of Edwards's doctrine of atonement is quite striking.

As we saw in a previous chapter, Edwards maintained that Adam and all his progeny form a single organic whole, Adam being the "root and stock" of the human tree, and all coming after him being the "buds and branches." Likewise, Edwards maintained that Christ and the church form a single organic whole, with Christ being the "root" and his saints being the "branches."[49] Edwards believed that the organic unity of Adam and the race explains how God can justly impute Adam's sins to us all. Likewise, he believed that the organic unity of Christ and the church explains how God can accept Christ's punishment on the church's behalf, and how he can count Christ's satisfaction and merit as theirs.[50] Moreover, Edwards maintained that the first Adam's sin involved a twofold offense: it injured God's *person* and *position*.[51] Thus, he also maintained that Christ's atone-

---

47. Edwards, *Miscellanies* no. 483, in *Works*, 13:526.
48. Edwards, *Miscellanies* no. 1146, in *Works*, 20:518.
49. Edwards, *Original Sin*, in *Works*, 3:386.
50. Mark Hamilton describes this teaching as the "realist-federalist amalgam" in "Jonathan Edwards on the Atonement," 397 n. 11.
51. Edwards's *Miscellanies* no. 319 offers one example of the twofold offense of sin: "God's infinite holiness and justice obliges him to exert his hatred and wrath against that that is infinitely odious, and an affront to an infinite majesty and authority." In *Works*,

ment necessarily involved a twofold work: he had to offer himself as a penal substitute for sinners, and he had to publicly vindicate God's government.

Herein lies the great difference between Edwards and his Grotian counterparts. While Edwards clearly saw a governmental component to the atonement, he did not emphasize that component *to the exclusion* of the doctrine of penal substitution as they did. For Edwards, the governmental component of Christ's atonement was necessary to answer the twofold offense of Adam's sin, truly making Christ the second Adam, but it was not the beginning and end of the atonement. It seems, then, that Edwards's contribution to the doctrine of atonement does indeed fall within the bounds of Reformed orthodoxy, and is distinct from the so-called governmental theory of atonement as developed by Hugo Grotius and Edwards's New Divinity successors; for governmental *language* is not a governmental *theory* until it has been separated from the doctrine of penal substitution.

The Atonement as an Act of Cosmic Victory

Edwards's doctrine of atonement contained another component common to his Reformation forebears, and that was the *Christus Victor* idea of the early church, meaning that Edwards also believed that Christ's atonement secured a great triumph over the forces of evil. An excellent example of this is present in one of his earliest *Miscellanies* entries. He begins by asking the question, "What rational ground of comfort is it that Christ has overcome the world?" His answer, in part, was the following:

> All the power of the world to hurt us is taken away by Christ, which would not have been taken away if it had not been for what Christ did on earth. So likewise, what he did took away the power of death and the devil; so that neither of them is able to hurt us so by worldly afflictions and likewise, what he did took away the power of death and the devil; so wicked men. It is certainly a rational ground of comfort, to think that our enemies have now no power to hurt us, and also that our Spouse has taken away this power.[52]

Edwards expressed a similar sentiment in his sermon entitled "Christ's Sacrifice," preached in the early 1720s. He wrote,

---

13:398.

52. Edwards, *Miscellanies* no. d, in *Works*, 13:165–66.

> The darling of Jehovah did not sweat blood for naught; he did [not] give himself cruelly to be slain and convicted to death for nothing. No, but redemption, eternal redemption, was purchased by it. Eternal redemption runs out of his veins. By this sweet-smelling savor of his sacrifice, he has made all in the nature that he assumed that receive him, acceptable in the sight of his Father. . . . By the pain that this Lamb of God endured when he was slain, all believers are delivered from eternal pain and shall receive eternal pleasure. By the shame that he was subject of is glory purchased. By dying he conquered death; by entering into the grave he destroyed the power of the grave. By his being tempted by [Satan] he forever disenabled him and crossed him, and has redeemed those that believe in him to God, by his blood, out of every tongue and kindred and nation to be with him, to behold his glory, and to sing hallelujahs to him forever and ever.[53]

THE EXTENT OF CHRIST'S ATONEMENT

The question of the atonement's nature leads naturally to the question of its extent, or better, its *intent*. On this point, Edwards again falls within the bounds of Reformed orthodoxy. He considered the matter from two angles. From the first angle, Edwards suggested that Christ's work was indeed for all men universally. In *Miscellanies* no. 424 he wrote,

> Christ did die for all in this sense, that all by his death have an opportunity of being [saved]; and he had that design in dying, that they should have that opportunity by it. For it was certainly a thing that God designed, that all men should have such an opportunity, or else they would not have it; and they have it by the death of Christ.[54]

Thus, Edwards affirmed that Christ died for all in the sense that anyone who comes to God through Christ will be saved. Beyond this, he may also be saying here that it is Christ's sacrifice that allows God to show patience toward all sinners for a time, giving them an "opportunity" to respond to God's grace with faith, rather than facing immediate condemnation. Regardless, this was his affirmation in his work *Original Sin*: "God deals with the generality of mankind, in their present state, far differently, on occasion

---

53. Edwards, "Christ's Sacrifice," in *Works*, 10:600.
54. Edwards, *Miscellanies* no. 424, in *Works*, 13:478. Brackets inserted by Stout. Edwards makes a similar statement in *Miscellanies* no. t, in *Works*, 13:174.

of the redemption by Jesus Christ, from what he otherwise would do: for, being capable subjects of saving mercy, they have a day of patience and grace, and innumerable temporal blessings bestowed on them; which, as the Apostle signifies (Acts 14:17), are testimonies of God's reconcilableness to sinful men, to put 'em upon seeking after God."[55]

From another angle, however, Edwards did see a connection between the eternal decrees of God and the work of atonement, thus limiting its intent to the elect. In *Miscellanies* no. 21 he writes, "This is certain, that God did not intend to save those by the death of Christ, that he certainly knew from all eternity he should not save by his death. Wherefore, it is certain that if he intended to save any by the death of Christ, he intended to save those whom he certainly knew he should save by his death."[56] In *Miscellanies* no. 25 he argues for the absurdity of universal intent, contending that if Christ died with the goal of making salvation *possible* for all, rather than *actual* for God's elect, then Christ must not have known for whom he was dying—because if he *did* foreknow which persons were going to believe, then he would have died with them in mind.[57] The implication is that one cannot have it both ways—one cannot have an omniscient Christ and an atonement with universal intent. Either Christ's foreknowledge must be jettisoned, or the idea of universal intent must be abandoned.

In another *Miscellanies* entry, dated very early in his ministry, Edwards argued for particular redemption in an atypical manner. Ignoring, for the sake of argument, the connection between God's knowledge and his decrees, Edwards suggested that we can establish the doctrine of particular redemption on the basis of Christ's omniscience alone. He writes,

> Universal redemption must be denied in the very sense of Calvinists themselves, whether predestination is acknowledged or no, if we acknowledge that Christ knows all things. If Christ certainly knows all things to come, he certainly knew, when he died, that there were such and such men that would never be the better for his death. And therefore, it was impossible that he should die with an intent to make them (particular persons) happy. For it is a right-down contradiction [to say that] he died with an intent to make them happy, when at the same time he knew they would not be happy.

---

55. Edwards, *Original Sin*, in *Works*, 3:415.
56. Edwards, *Miscellanies* no. 21, in *Works*, 13:211.
57. Edwards, *Miscellanies* no. 25, in *Works*, 13:212.

The Vital Content of Edwards's Doctrine of Atonement

He concludes: "this is all that Calvinists mean when they say that Christ did not die for all: that he did not die intending and designing that such and such particular persons should be the better for it." As he closes this entry, he expresses solidarity with Arminians who teach that Christ's death creates an opportunity for all to believe, since Calvinists affirm this as well. Nevertheless, he insists that saying the cross gives all men an *opportunity* to be saved is not the same thing as saying that Christ died *with the goal* of saving all men. Christ did *not* die with the *intent* of making all men "the better" for his death.[58]

Another significant passage on the extent of the atonement is from Edwards's sermon on Galatians 2:20. He begins by placing Christ's atonement in the broader context of the covenant of redemption, in which God the Father promises Christ a specific number of individuals as the reward for Christ's sufferings. Edwards maintains that Christ was told exactly who those men were, before the world began. Next, Edwards quotes several passages from the Gospel of John that affirm the definite intent of the atonement. He quotes John 6:37, for example, which says, "all that the Father giveth me shall come to come to me." Edwards explains that from eternity past Christ looked upon the elect as his "own possession and reward, and his crown. He took delight in them before the earth was created. He looks upon them as his before they actually believe." "Christ did as it were write down the names of his people from eternity," he says. And when Christ died, "he had the names of every one of them upon his heart." After discussing the Arminian contention that Christ died for all in the same way, he again turns to his argument from Christ's omniscience. He writes,

> It matters not in this controversy whether we suppose an absolute decree or no, if we only allow that God knows . . . future things before they come to pass as he declares he does in his word and which no Christians pretend to deny. . . . And if they say that nothing else is intended when they say that Christ died for all then that through his death all have the offer of salvation, so that they may have salvation if they will accept of salvation . . . if that be all that is intended, they are against none that are called Christians, who

---

58. Edwards, *Miscellanies* no. *t*, in *Works*, 13:174. Edwards undoubtedly felt the need to hedge his statements on particular redemption because of the theological milieu in which he lived. As he wrote in another place, "the term 'Calvinist' is in these days, among most, a term of greater reproach than the term 'Arminian.'" *Freedom of the Will*, in *Works*, 1:131.

Part 2: Atonement in the Works of Jonathan Edwards

own that by Christ's death all that live under the gospel have the offer of salvation.

Moving to his next argument, Edwards makes the case that if a person rejects particular redemption, he must also deny the notion that Christ's atonement was guaranteed to have success. Here is why: if the application of the atonement is left ultimately to the will of man, rather than to the will of God, Edwards says, then the possibility always remains that the cross would have no positive effect at all. And then finally, in the last part of his sermon, Edwards appealed to the numerous other Scripture texts that lend support to particular redemption, including Ephesians 5:25; John 10:14–15; and John 17:9.[59]

Many other sermons could be cited to demonstrate Edwards's commitment to particular redemption. In his sermon on Romans 2:10, he states explicitly that "God gave Christ to die for the elect." And in his sermon on Isaiah 53:11, he says, "such delight doth Christ take in the salvation and eternal blessedness of those that he has loved, that he is fully satisfied with it as reward enough for all the suffering he has undergone." And from his sermon on Romans 5:7–8: "Christ's love was such to his elect that he came down from heaven, he left the bosom of the Father, he laid aside his glory and came down to dwell on earth." And from his sermon on Romans 8:29–30: "the going of Christ to die for the elect is the principal manifestation of his [the Father's] love to 'em." And, from a sermon on Revelation 14:3: "He has died for them [i.e., the elect] and not for the world."[60]

In *Miscellanies* no. 781, Edwards even uses the doctrine of particular redemption as a motive for evangelism. He writes, "we ought to hate no man, because there is room to hope that Christ has suffered and satisfied for his sins; and therefore, we should endeavor to bring him to Christ."[61] These statements clearly put Edwards at odds with the post-Enlightenment theologians and argue strongly for his place in the mainstream of Reformed orthodoxy.

---

59. Edwards, sermon no. 91, in *Works Online*, vol. 43. The block quote offered above represents my own edited version of Edwards's manuscript, which, given the nature of the manuscript, was necessarily paraphrastic at times.

60. Unpublished sermons, quoted in Gerstner, *Rational Biblical Theology of Jonathan Edwards*, 2:435.

61. Edwards, *Miscellanies* no. 781, in *Works*, 18:450–52.

The Vital Content of Edwards's Doctrine of Atonement

HOW CHRIST'S ATONEMENT IS APPROPRIATED BY THE ELECT

On the question of how Christ's atonement is appropriated by the elect, Edwards's answer is virtually indistinguishable from his Reformed orthodox predecessors, though his manner of explanation is unique. Like them, he asserts that the benefits of the atonement are received by faith alone. "Faith is the soul's active uniting with Christ," he says, "or is the very act of unition, on their part." He argues that if two persons are to be legally regarded as one, "there should be a mutual act of both, that each should receive the other, as actively joining themselves to one another." Christ, of course, reached out to his elect by loving them and dying for them. It is for the individual, now, to reach out to Christ. "God . . . treats men as reasonable creatures," Edwards asserts, "capable of act, and choice; and hence sees it fit that they only, that are one with Christ by their own act, should be looked upon as one in law." Edwards maintains that "it is something really in them, and between them, uniting them, that is the ground of the suitableness of their being accounted as one by the Judge," that he might "accept the satisfaction and merits of the one, for the other, as if it were their satisfaction and merits."[62]

Upon exercising faith, all the benefits of the atonement are imputed to the elect. In *Miscellanies* no. 1237 he uses an analogy to explain how this can justly take place: if a man dies in the service of his country, Edwards says, the man's heirs may receive a financial gift from the public treasury. Additionally, estates may transfer from one to another upon a man's death. How much more, then, should God be able to permit this for sinners by his grace, who are one with Christ by faith?[63]

CONCLUSION

In conclusion, the vital content of Edwards's doctrine of atonement was clearly inherited from the Reformed orthodox tradition. His basic structure was covenantal, he affirmed the absolute necessity of the atonement, he included the concept of substitutionary penal satisfaction in his understanding of the atonement's nature, he argued for particular redemption,

---

62. Edwards, *Justification by Faith Alone*, in *Works*, 19:158.
63. Edwards, *Miscellanies* no. 1237, in *Works*, 23:172.

and he declared that the benefits of the atonement are appropriated by faith alone.

Edwards did muse quite extensively about the *mechanics* of the atonement, as well as Christ's psychological state during the crucifixion, but nothing that he said should be interpreted as conflicting with the penal substitutionary view. They were merely additions, or supplements, to the doctrine. They were attempts fill some of the lacunae of the doctrine, without changing the basic Reformed model. His doctrine of atonement is classic Reformed orthodoxy, examined and expressed within an eighteenth-century New England context.

Chapter 7

Additional Emphases in Edwards's Doctrine of Atonement

THE BASIC FRAMEWORK OF Edwards's doctrine of atonement has been assembled, and the vital content has been put into place. Even so, the full substance of Edwards's doctrine has not yet been presented. What follows in this brief chapter is a collection of additional emphases in the Edwards corpus concerning his theology of atonement. These are found chiefly in his sermons, though a few ideas are also contained in his private writings. Continuing the puzzle analogy from previous chapters, these thoughts may be compared to the glass and frame that encapsulate the assembled puzzle. These final thoughts adorn Edwards's doctrine of atonement, putting the finishing touches upon it. They include his thoughts on the atonement as a loving act, a self-denying act, a voluntary act, and a beautiful act.

THE ATONEMENT AS A LOVING ACT

What motivated Christ to enter into that covenant of redemption with the Father, accepting the almost impossibly difficult terms, and offering himself in atonement for sin? Edwards says that Christ was motivated entirely by love—which brings his doctrine of atonement full circle. From all eternity the members of the Trinity have existed in a state of pure love. God's decision to create was from the overflow of his Trinitarian love. After man's fall, Christ came in love to restore what had been broken.

First and foremost, Christ was motivated by his love for the Father, but he also came out of love for his elect. Edwards Amasa Park notes the unique emphasis on love in Edwards's doctrine of atonement when he writes, "[Edwards] not only represents love as the first motive prompting our Redeemer to undertake his mission, but he also represents a sympathetic love as one principle means of the Redeemer's suffering, after he had undertaken the work of redeeming us."[1]

Edwards discusses Christ's love for the Father in *Miscellanies* no. 327(a). He asserts once more that the "highest glory" of the Trinity is the "infinite love" that exists between Father and Son. It seemed fitting to the Godhead, therefore, to showcase that mutual love to the world. This is what the cross achieved. "The infinite love of the Father to the Son is . . . manifested, in that for [the Son's] sake he would forgive an infinite debt, would be reconciled with and receive into his favor and to his enjoyment those that had rebelled against him and injured his infinite majesty." The infinite love of the Son to the Father is seen in the Son's "infinitely abasing himself for the vindicating of [the Father's] authority and the honor of his majesty." "When God had a mind to save men," Edwards writes, "Christ infinitely laid out himself that the honor of God's majesty might be safe and that God's glory might be advanced."[2] These statements bring both major emphases of Edwards's doctrine of atonement into focus. The Father loved the Son so much that he was willing to forgive those for whom Christ had become a penal substitute. And, the Son loved the Father so much that he could not bear the thought of the Father's dishonor. So he came, and perfectly obeyed the divine law, and died to vindicate the Father's rightful place as moral governor of the world.

In *Miscellanies* no. 483 Edwards stresses the Father's love for the Son once more. He writes that "the divine excellency of Christ and the love of the Father to him, is the life and soul of all that Christ did and suffered in the work of redemption. Indeed, men have their sins pardoned for the sake of the divine excellency of Christ, and we are accepted into God's favor and have a title to eternal life for the sake of Christ, because the Father infinitely loves him." This means that God's willingness to reconcile with sinners is not fundamentally because he loves the sinner, but because he loves the Son who died in their stead. Indeed, God's love for the Son is what causes him to love the sinner.[3]

---

1. Park, *Atonement*, xxxviii–xxxix.

2. Edwards, *Miscellanies* no. 327(a), in *Works*, 13:406.

3. Edwards, *Miscellanies* no. 483, in *Works*, 13:524. The same point is made in *Miscellanies* no. b, in *Works*, 13:164–65.

Additional Emphases in Edwards's Doctrine of Atonement

Of course, the atonement also displays Christ's deep love for the lost. In his sermon on Galatians 2:20, Edwards declares, "[Christ] had a dying love to every particular believer . . . to all that have been since Christ was upon the earth amongst all Christianized nations and to all that shall be to the end of the world. [Furthermore,] Christ don't only love them after they actually believe in him and love him, but the apostle tells us in 1 John 4:19, 'we love him because he first loved us,' and the shedding of his blood is the fruit of this love." He goes on:

> The love of Christ is not the less to one because there are a great many that are loved. . . . 'Tis no hindrance to the entireness and strength of Christ's love that there are such multitudes. . . . Our love is finite and may be divided, but the love of Christ is boundless. . . . [There] is no emptying of the fountain of his love because the fountain is infinite. His dying love is not divided but is as it were wholly exercised towards every particular believer.[4]

In his notes on Leviticus 14:12–18 from his *Blank Bible*, Edwards asserts that Christ's love for God and sinners is the very thing that renders his atoning work effective. He writes, "the sacrifice of Christ was offered up to God with the Spirit, with divine love, love to God and love to men, which sanctified the sacrifice and made it effectual." Drawing on an Old Testament analogy, he continues: "Both the blood and the oil were first offered to God before they were applied to the leper. So not only is Christ's blood first presented to God before 'tis applied to the sinner, but the spirit of love that he has without measure, first flows out to God before it flows out to the sinner and be communicated to him in sanctification."[5]

Connecting this quote to previous statements in this study, Edwards's meaning is clear. Christ's love for God and men made his work effectual in the sense that it was his infinite love for his elect that created the bond of union between them, enabling his payment to be counted as theirs. And, it was his love for the Father's honor that caused him to agree to an incarnation and atonement in the first place. More than that, it was his love for the Father that rendered the atonement pleasing to God. Just as God was not moved by empty ritual in the old dispensation, so too is he unmoved by anything short of a loving act in the present age. And finally, it is the Father's love for the Son that prompts him to reconcile with those sinners for whom Christ died, for

---

4. Edwards, sermon no. 91, in *Works Online*, vol. 43. This sermon is currently only available in a rough format. The quotations above represent my own edition of the text.

5. Edwards, Leviticus 14:12–18, in *Works*, 24:254.

if Christ loved them enough to substitute himself for them, then the Father must love them enough to reconcile with them. Thus, for Edwards, divine love is the alpha and omega of Christ's atoning work.

THE ATONEMENT AS A VOLUNTARY ACT

Edwards preached the sermon entitled "The Free and Voluntary Suffering and Death of Christ" in 1738.[6] The sermon, based on John 10:18, begins with a provocative statement: "Christ did not kill himself; the death of Christ was a murder." Yet, Edwards insists, it was a murder that Christ acquiesced to "freely" and "voluntarily."

The idea that Christ's sacrifice was voluntary was very important to Edwards, so he spent a considerable amount of time establishing its truth, arguing particularly for the idea on the basis of Christ's nature as the God-man. Beginning with Christ's divine nature, Edwards insisted that Christ must have suffered voluntarily because Deity simply cannot be coerced. Deity is by definition perfectly free. Additionally, Deity is not *subject* to anyone or anything. Since Christ is fully divine, he could not have been coerced into his incarnation and passion. It must have been his free choice. Here, Edwards's covenant theology again comes into prominence. He argues that Christ's incarnation and death were the result of the eternal covenant of redemption between Father and Son. Being a covenant, the Father did not command the Son to accept his terms; instead, the terms were settled by mutual agreement. Christ's atoning work only became an imperative *after* the covenant was ratified. Therefore, Christ's death was a free decision.

Third, Christ proved that his death was voluntary through the many prophetic statements he made before the time of his death arrived. Fourth, it is proven by all of the Old Testament "types and shadows" that represented his death, such as the animal sacrifices. Edwards insisted that these types and shadows were appointed by Christ himself, before the commencement of his earthly ministry. Fifth, Edwards argued the voluntary nature of Christ's death on the basis of the incarnation itself. Why would Deity put on humanity, if not to experience death? Sixth, Edwards argued that Christ's decision to enter the world in such a lowly estate, and to remain in that state for the duration of his life, demonstrated that he had come to suffer.

6. Edwards, "The Free and Voluntary Suffering and Death of Christ," in *Works* 19:491–514.

Additional Emphases in Edwards's Doctrine of Atonement

Edwards also argued his premise from the side of Christ's humanity. As a man, Edwards said, Christ "took great delight in the thoughts of his sufferings for sinners, because he knew that that would be a thing greatly to God's glory." Christ knew that his death would glorify God's authority, holiness, justice, and grace; his *person*, as well as his *position*. Second, the human Christ delighted in the thought of the "testimony of his love to his elect," which would be manifested by his death on their behalf. Third, as a man, Christ knew that his penal, substitutionary death would bring about the salvation of sinners. Edwards wrote, "it was exceeding pleasant to him to think how the justice of God would be satisfied, and perishing souls would have safety and deliverance through his suffering."

According to Edwards, Christ's willingness to submit himself to death on behalf of sinners was tested on two occasions. These tests were necessary, he said, to *confirm* the voluntary nature of his sufferings. The first test was in the Garden of Gethsemane, where it appears that Christ was given "an extraordinary view" of the sufferings that were to come. This extraordinary view was necessary because Christ's sufferings could not truly be considered voluntary if he did not have a full understanding of what he would have to endure. The second test consisted of Christ receiving "a great and extraordinary view" of mankind's sinfulness. This allowed him to see how unworthy man was of Christ's atonement, giving Christ an opportunity to decide whether he was willing to offer himself for them. Seeing that Christ passed these tests, Edwards said, we can be confident that the death he endured was an entirely free and voluntary act, meaning that he did not merely fulfill a duty, but performed a positive work that could achieve the salvation of sinners.

This last statement explains why the voluntary nature of Christ's sacrifice was so important to him. If Christ's sacrifice had not been entirely voluntary, it could not have made satisfaction for sin. Edwards makes this point with great force in his sermon "The Sacrifice of Christ Acceptable," based on Psalm 40:6–8.[7] He argues that if Christ submitted to death simply because the Father told him to do so, then his death would have only fulfilled a duty; it would not have made satisfaction for human sin.

Even in his discussion of the voluntary nature of Christ, then, we see the dual emphasis of Edwards's doctrine of atonement coming through.

---

7. Edwards, "The Sacrifice of Christ Acceptable," in *Works*, 14:437–58. Many of the thoughts contained in this sermon were first set down in *Notes on Scripture* no. 171, in *Works*, 15:99–100.

Why did Christ volunteer for this task? Because it thrilled him to think that his substitutionary death would secure the salvation of sinners, and because he longed to vindicate the moral government of God. The two concepts came together in his doctrine of Christ's death.

THE ATONEMENT AS A SELF-DENYING ACT

Christ's atonement was a loving and voluntary act to secure the salvation of sinners and vindicate the government of God. It was also a supreme act of self-denial. Edwards's sermon entitled "Christ's Sacrifice an Inducement to His Ministers," preached at the installation service of his friend Edward Billing in 1754, provides a good example of this theme.[8] He begins with the premise that "it is a greater thing for one that is originally in a very happy state to be willing to descend into a state of affliction and torment, than another: the self-denial in it is greater in proportion to the degree of happiness he descends from." His argument is that since Christ enjoyed the highest and happiest state imaginable, it must follow that the self-denial required of Christ to submit to the cross was unprecedented.

Edwards explains that Christ retained the memory of his preincarnate happiness even as he walked this earth, which made his self-sacrifice all the greater. He points to passages like John 17:5 to prove his contention. The verse reads, "And now, O Father, glorify thou me with thine own self with the glory which I had with thee before the world was." The glory that he enjoyed before the world, Edwards says, was "the enjoyment of his Father's love so that he knew by experience the infinite value of that love." This is why he cried out on the cross, "My God, my God, why hast thou forsaken me?" He knew the infinite depths of his Father's comfort; to have that now replaced with wrath was almost more than he could bear.

The depth of Christ's self-denial is further seen in the fact that his shed blood was truly "God's own blood," which means that it was the blood of one "infinitely above any need of us," "infinitely above any need of

---

8. Edwards, "Christ's Sacrifice an Inducement to His Ministers," in *Works*, 25:653–75. Rev. Billing had been dismissed from his previous church in 1752 because of his vocal support of Edwards's position on the Lord's Supper at the council convened in Northampton. He had apparently participated in the council against the wishes of his congregation, and had supported Edwards at the council despite his congregation's rejection of Edwards's views. As the editors of this installation sermon state, "when Billing finally found another ministerial post at Greenfield, Massachusetts, in 1754, it was particularly appropriate to have Edwards preach his installation sermon."

anything." Christ did not need to redeem sinful men in order to be happy. He was eternally and infinitely happy in the Godhead. "Indeed," Edwards says, "the eternal, infinite happiness of the divine being seems to be social, consisting in the infinitely blessed union and society of the persons of the Trinity, so that they are happy in one another . . . [they] gave one another happiness as [they] derived happiness from one another." As part of that eternal, blessed Godhead, Christ could not be hurt by "our sin and misery." "Nor did he need that we should be made holy and happy; he needs not our presence with him in heaven, nor can he be profited by anything that we can be or do there." As he could gain nothing by his atoning work, that work must have been an act of pure self-sacrifice, pure self-denial.

THE ATONEMENT AS A BEAUTIFUL ACT

Edwards's stress on the aesthetic is one of the features that distinguishes him from other theologians.[9] We saw hints of this in a previous chapter, where Edwards discussed God's desire to arrange all things "beautifully." McClymond and McDermott, in their recent work, *The Theology of Jonathan Edwards*, point out the many places where the beauty of Christ's atonement is emphasized in the Edwards corpus. Quoting Edwards, they explain that through Christ's atonement, the "brightest effulgence" of his "beauty and amiable excellency" are put on display, for through it the elect come to see that "Jesus Christ is infinitely the most beautiful and glorious object in the world," more beautiful than "the sun in his meridian glory." Further, Edwards speaks of the beauty of Christ's righteousness, a "lovely virtue" imputed to the elect. "'Tis the lovely robe, and robe of love, with which they are covered," he writes. Edwards also speaks of the beauty of the saints clothed in Christ's righteousness: "Christ gives it to them, and puts it upon them, and by the beauty of this robe recommends 'em to the favor and delight of God the Father, as well as of all heaven besides." This beauty, Edwards says, covers over the saints' "deformity," rendering them as lovely as their Savior.[10] These statements are only possible, of course, if Edwards believed in the doctrine of penal substitution. It is by means of Christ's substitutionary act that their sins are imputed to him, and his righteousness to them.

---

9. For an excellent volume on this subject, see Strachan and Sweeney, *Jonathan Edwards on Beauty*.

10. McClymond and McDermott, *Theology of Jonathan Edwards*, 252.

CONCLUSION

As we near the end of our study, we see how doctrine and affection wove together in Edwards's doctrine of atonement. The nature of Christ's work is not something just to occupy the mind, but also something to stir one's sense of wonder. In the discourses herein considered, Edwards encourages the reader to think about the fact that Christ's work was motivated entirely by love, this being the very definition of the Deity. Likewise, it was offered freely and voluntarily, so that none should think that Christ was coerced in any way. The atonement was also a supremely sacrificial act, seeing that the Trinitarian God did not need men for fellowship or happiness. Finally, the atonement was a beautiful act. It displayed the loveliness of the Son of God as never seen before, and it offered the saints of God beauty for ashes.

Conclusion

What Is Jonathan Edwards's Legacy on the Atonement?

JONATHAN EDWARDS'S LEGACY IS remarkable. By the time he finished his earthly course, he had pastored three churches, raised a large family, led a Great Awakening, mentored aspiring ministers, presided over a college, and produced a vast treasury of theological literature. To the present day, his ideas are discussed and disseminated by a virtual army of pastors, scholars, and laypeople. Edwards's contribution to the doctrine of atonement is a part of that legacy, though it has not yet received the attention that it is due.

The aim of the present study has been to correct this imbalance by surveying Edwards's collected works and determining what he believed about the atonement. Our conclusion is that Edwards's doctrine of atonement was within the mainstream of classic Reformed orthodoxy, examined and expressed within an eighteenth-century New England context. While Edwards did use governmental language in his discussions of the atonement, this was not at the expense of the doctrine of substitutionary penal satisfaction and did not conflict with it. In fact, what this governmental language did for Edwards was to add *symmetry* to his doctrine of atonement. As we have seen, Edwards believed that Adam's relationship to humanity and Christ's relationship to the church are parallel: just as Adam and his natural seed form a single organic whole, so too do Christ and the church. Edwards believed that this organic unity explains the justice of the doctrine of imputation. Because Adam and his natural seed form a single organism, the sin of Adam may justly be reckoned to all. Likewise, because Christ and his church form a single organism, God can justly impute the sins of the elect to Christ, and Christ's righteousness to them. His doctrinal stance was, as Mark Hamilton notes, a "realist-federalist amalgam."[1] This also explains Edwards's dual emphasis on the atonement. He believed that Adam's sin involved a twofold offense: it defied God's character *and* his government. Therefore, Christ's atonement necessarily involved a twofold work: he had to offer himself as a penal substitute for sinners, and he had to publicly vindicate God's government. Both were necessary for sin's penalty to be satisfied.

Herein lies the great difference between Edwards and his Grotian/Arminian/Rationalist counterparts. While Edwards clearly saw a governmental component to the atonement, he did not emphasize that component to the exclusion of the doctrine of penal substitution as they did. Penal substitution remained the center and hinge of his system. Yet, the governmental component of Christ's atonement was necessary to answer Adam's twofold offense, truly making Christ the "second Adam."

This twofold emphasis also sets Edwards apart from the atonement theory of the New Divinity men. A side-by-side comparison of Edwards's view with theirs is particularly eye-opening. For this, we return to the nine-point summary of the New Divinity's position as articulated by Edwards Amasa Park.[2] First, Park said, the New Divinity believed that "our Lord suffered pains which were substituted for the penalty of the law, and may be called punishment in the more general sense of that word, but were not, strictly and literally, the penalty which the law had threatened." Edwards clearly disagreed. He understood Christ's death to be exactly that which the law had threatened, "strictly and literally." While Edwards certainly had other things to say about Christ's death, such as it being an act to honor God's law, these additional statements were never at the expense of the former.

Secondly, the New Divinity believed that "the sufferings of our Lord satisfied the general justice of God, but did not satisfy his distributive justice." Edwards, of course, affirmed both truths. He believed that Christ died for the sake of God's rectoral justice, but also for his distributive justice.

Thirdly, the New Divinity taught that "the humiliation, pains, and death of our Redeemer were equivalent in meaning to the punishment threatened in the moral law, and thus they satisfied Him who is determined to maintain the honor of his law, but they did not satisfy the demands of

---

1. Hamilton, "Jonathan Edwards on the Atonement," 397 n. 11.
2. Park, *Atonement*, x–xi.

the law itself for our punishment." Once again, Edwards could not accept this statement. While he did teach that Christ's death served to uphold the honor of God's law, he did not deny that Christ's death also satisfied the real demands of the law. God did not relax the law's demands when he accepted Christ's sacrifice; rather, he accepted Christ's sacrifice precisely because it was fully equivalent to what the law required.

Fourthly, the New Divinity taught that "the active obedience . . . of Christ was honorable to the law, but was not a work of supererogation, performed by our Substitute, and then transferred and imputed to us, so as to satisfy the requisitions of the law for our own active obedience." Here again, Edwards said otherwise. He argued that human salvation depends upon Christ's satisfaction and merit, and he taught that Christ earned his merit by living a righteous life, which becomes the possession of the elect by means of imputation when they exercise saving faith.

Fifthly, the New Divinity taught that "the law and the distributive justice of God, although honored by the life and death of Christ, will yet eternally demand the punishment of every one who has sinned." This too Edwards denied. He taught that the love that exists between Christ and believers unites them together into a single entity, so that Christ's death is their death, and his merit their merit. Thus, the demand of punishment has been utterly set aside for those who are in Christ.

Sixthly, the New Divinity taught that "the atonement rendered it consistent and desirable for God to save all who exercise evangelical faith, yet it did not render it obligatory on Him, in distribute justice to save them." Edwards could not accept this statement either. While agreeing that the atonement gives all men everywhere the opportunity to repent, believe, and be saved, Edwards also believed that God was under obligation to save the elect because of the atonement. God was obliged in justice, because the full penalty for sins had been paid for the elect; and he was obliged in love, seeing that he could not reject those for whom his beloved Son had shown the last full measure of devotion.

Seventhly, the New Divinity taught that "the atonement was designed for the welfare of all men; to make the eternal salvation of all men possible; to remove all the obstacles which the honor of the law and of distributive justice presented against the salvation of the non-elect as well as the elect." While Edwards was quick to affirm that the atonement did provide benefits to the non-elect, allowing God to show patience toward them and to give them an opportunity to believe, he did not accept the notion of *universal intent* in the atonement. Christ did not die to make the salvation of all men possible. He died to secure the salvation of the elect. This is because Christ died as a penal substitute for the elect.

Eighthly, the New Divinity taught that "the atonement does not constitute the reason why some men are regenerated, and others not, but this reason is found only in the sovereign, electing will of God." This statement would seem to conflict with the covenant theology of Jonathan Edwards. Edwards tied both God's election of sinners and Christ's atonement for sinners to the eternal covenant of redemption between Father and Son. They therefore cannot be considered apart from each other, but are simply two sides to the same agreement. And the Holy Spirit's application of the atonement, in the form of regeneration, cannot be separated from the others either, for the covenant of grace is simply the historical outworking of the covenant of redemption.

Ninthly, the New Divinity taught that "the atonement is *useful* on men's account, and in order to furnish new motives to holiness, but it is *necessary* on God's account, and in order to *enable* him, as a consistent Ruler, to pardon any, even the smallest sin, and therefore to bestow on sinners any, even the smallest favor." Edwards may have accepted some of that statement, but not all. Specifically, he would have qualified the opening of the statement by saying that the atonement furnishes new motives to *believers* to be holy, but he would have rejected the notion that the unregenerate could be spiritually persuaded in such a manner. Further, Christ's work did not merely give God the ability to "pardon . . . sin," but actually paid sin's price.

As was noted previously, governmental language only becomes a governmental theory of the atonement when it is separated from the doctrine of penal substitution. Because Edwards brought together both substitutionary and non-substitutionary components into a single, unified system, his contribution belongs within the stream of Reformed orthodoxy. The question remains, however, as to how much responsibility Edwards bears for his successors' modified governmental theory. While this was not the central question of the study, a brief answer is in order. In this writer's opinion, Edwards does bear some, but not all, of the responsibility for the doctrinal trajectory of his successors. While he himself was classically Reformed, he may not have sufficiently guarded against the separation of the substitutionary and governmental components of his system, giving his disciples some impetus for their new trajectory. His decision to endorse Joseph Bellamy's work *True Religion Delineated* illustrates the point. Edwards may have

Conclusion

agreed with the governmental language of the book as far as it went, but by not encouraging his disciple to include a presentation of the substitutionary aspect of the atonement, he may have unwittingly encouraged him to abandon it. It is also conceivable that Edwards's private writings, which fell into the hands of his disciples after he died, could have encouraged their new direction. His notes often used governmental language, without integrating those thoughts into his total system.

Yet, Edwards does not bear all of the responsibility. He is not responsible for how his words may have been misunderstood by his successors after they took possession of his manuscripts. And, we must not discount the elements of human nature and cultural context in considering the trajectory of the Edwardeans. Their interest in human reason, combined with their desire to present the faith in a reasonable way to those of their "enlightened" age, could have influenced their theological direction.

Bibliography

Allison, Greg. "A History of the Doctrine of the Atonement." *Southern Baptist Journal of Theology* 11:2 (Summer 2007) 4-19.
Aloisi, John. "'His Flesh for Our Flesh': The Doctrine of Atonement in the Second Century." *Detroit Baptist Seminary Journal* 14 (2009) 23-44.
Ames, William. *The Marrow of Theology*. Translated with an introduction by John Dykstra Eusden. Grand Rapids: Baker, 1968.
Anselm. *Cur Deus Homo?* London: Unwin Brothers, n.d.
Aquinas, Thomas. *Summa Theologica*. Vol. 16. 2nd rev. ed. Translated by the Fathers of the English Dominican Province. London: Burns Oates & Washbourne, 1926.
Arminius, Jacobus. *The Works of Arminius*. Translated by James Nichols and William Nichols. 3 vols. Grand Rapids: Baker, 1991.
Athanasius. *On the Incarnation*. Grand Rapids: Christian Classics Ethereal Library. http://www.ccel.org/ccel/athanasius/incarnation.
Aulen, Gustaf. *Christus Victor: An Historical Study of the Three Main Types of the Idea of the Atonement*. New York: MacMillan, 1969.
Beeke, Joel R., and Mark Jones. *A Puritan Theology: Doctrine for Life*. Grand Rapids: Reformation Heritage, 2012.
Berkhof, Louis. *The History of Christian Doctrines*. Carlisle, PA: Banner of Truth Trust, 1978.
Breitenback, William. "The Consistent Calvinism of the New Divinity Movement." *William and Mary Quarterly* 41:2 (April 1984) 241-64.
Calvin, John. *Institutes of the Christian Religion*. Edited by John T. McNeill, translated by Ford Lewis Battles. 2 vols. Philadelphia: Westminster, 1960.
Cherry, Conrad. *The Theology of Jonathan Edwards: A Reappraisal*. Indianapolis: Indiana University Press, 1966.
Conforti, Joseph. *Samuel Hopkins and the New Divinity*. Grand Rapids: Eerdmans, 1981.
Crabtree, A. B. *Jonathan Edwards' View of Man: A Study in Eighteenth Century Calvinism*. Wallington, England: Religious Education Press, 1948.
Crawford, Brandon. "Jonathan Edwards: Theologian of God's Glory in Christ." *Puritan Reformed Journal* 7:1 (January 2015) 120-42.

Bibliography

Crisp, Oliver. "Penal Non-Substitution." *Journal of Theological Studies* 59:1 (April 2008) 140–68.

Crisp, Oliver, and Douglas A. Sweeny, eds. *After Jonathan Edwards: The Courses of the New England Theology.* New York: Oxford University Press, 2012.

Dexter, Franklin B., ed. *The Literary Diary of Ezra Stiles.* Vol. 3 New York: Scribner, 1901.

Dodd, Elizabeth. *Marriage to a Difficult Man: The Uncommon Union of Jonathan and Sarah Edwards.* Laurel, MS: Audubon, 2004.

Dwight, Sereno. *Memoirs of Jonathan Edwards.* In *The Works of Jonathan Edwards*, vol. 1. Edinburgh: Banner of Truth Trust, 1974.

Dwight, Timothy. *Theology Explained and Defended.* 5 vols. London: Forgotten Books, 2012.

Edwards, Jonathan. *A History of the Work of Redemption.* Reprint ed. Carlisle, PA: Banner of Truth Trust, 2003.

———. *The Works of Jonathan Edwards.* Vols. 1–26. Perry Miller, general editor. New Haven, CT: Yale University Press, 1957–2008.

———. *The Works of Jonathan Edwards Online.* Vols. 27–73. New Haven, CT: Jonathan Edwards Center, Yale University, 2008–2016. http://edwards.yale.edu.

Eusden, John. *Puritans, Lawyers, and Politics in Early Seventeenth-Century England.* New Haven, CT: Yale University Press, 1958.

Eusebius. *Ecclesiastical History.* Translated with an introduction by Christian Frederick Cruse. Grand Rapids: Baker, 1962.

Flavel, John. *The Works of John Flavel.* Vol. 1. Carlisle, PA: Banner of Truth Trust, 1997.

George, Timothy. *Theology of the Reformers.* Nashville: Broadman, 1988.

Gerstner, John. *Jonathan Edwards: A Mini-Theology.* Morgan, PA: Soli Deo Gloria, 1996.

———. *The Rational Biblical Theology of Jonathan Edwards.* 3 vols. Orlando, FL: Ligonier, 1992.

Gomes, Alan W. "*De Jesu Christo Servatore*: Faustus Socinus on the Satisfaction of Christ." *Westminster Theological Journal* 55 (1993) 209–31.

———. "*De Jesu Christo Servatore* Part III: Historical Introduction, Translation, and Critical Notes." PhD diss., Fuller Theological Seminary, 1990.

———. "Faustus Socinus and John Calvin on the Merits of Christ." *Reformation & Renaissance Review* 12:2–3 (2010) 189–205.

Grensted, L. W., ed. *The Atonement in History and in Life: A Volume of Essays.* London: SPCK, 1929.

———. *A Short History of the Doctrine of the Atonement.* Manchester: University of Manchester Press, 1920.

Grotius, Hugo. *A Defence of the Catholic Faith Concerning the Satisfaction of Christ, Against Faustus Socinus.* Translated by Frank Hugh Foste. Andover: W. F. Draper, 1889.

Guelzo, Allen C. *Edwards on the Will: A Century of American Theological Debate.* Middletown, CT: Wesleyan University Press, 1989.

Hamilton, S. Mark. "Jonathan Edwards on the Atonement." *International Journal of Systematic Theology* 15:2 (October 2013) 394–415.

Haroutunian, Joseph G. "Jonathan Edwards: Theologian of the Great Commandment." *Theology Today* 1:3 (1944) 361–77.

Hartog, Paul. *Polycarp and the New Testament: The Occasion, Rhetoric, Theme, and Unity of the Epistle to the Philippians and Its Allusions to New Testament Literature.* Tubingen: Mohr, 2002.

Bibliography

Haykin, Michael. *Jonathan Edwards: The Holy Spirit in Revival.* Webster, NY: Evangelical Press, 2005.

Hicks, John Mark. "The Theology of Grace in the Theology of Jacobus Arminius and Philip Van Limborch: A Study in the Development of Seventeenth-Century Dutch Arminianism." PhD diss., Westminster Theological Seminary, 1985.

Hillerbrand, Hans J. *Men and Ideas in the Sixteenth Century.* Chicago: Rand McNally, 1969.

Holmes, Stephen R. *God of Grace and God of Glory: An Account of the Theology of Jonathan Edwards.* Grand Rapids: Eerdmans, 2000.

Hopkins, Samuel. *A Bold Push: In a Letter to the Author of a Late Pamphlet, Intitled, Fair Play.* Boston: Edes and Gill, 1758.

———. *The Life and Character of the Late Reverend, Learned, and Pious Mr. Jonathan Edwards.* Northampton: Andrew Wright, for S. and E. Butler, 1804.

Jeffery, Steve, Michael Ovey, and Andrew Sach. *Pierced for Our Transgressions: Rediscovering the Glory of Penal Substitution.* Wheaton, IL: Crossway, 2007.

Jinkins, Michael. "Atonement and the Character of God: A Comparative Study in the Theology of Atonement in Jonathan Edwards and John McLeod Campbell." PhD, diss., University of Aberdeen, 1989.

Kerr, Hugh T, ed. *A Compend of Luther's Theology.* Philadelphia: Westminster, 1966.

Lee, Sang Hyun. *The Philosophical Theology of Jonathan Edwards.* Princeton, NJ: Princeton University Press, 1988.

Lightfoot, J. B. *Saint Paul's Epistle to the Philippians.* Grand Rapids: Zondervan, 1953.

Limborch, Philippus van. *A Compleat System, or Body of Divinity, Both Speculative and Practical, Founded on Scripture and Reason.* 2 vols. Translated by William Jones. London: John Darby, 1713. ECCO. http://find.galegroup.com/ecco/start.do?prodId=ECCO&userGroupName=gran17045.

Luther, Martin. *Luther's Works.* Vol. 26. Translated by Jaroslav Pelikan. St. Louis: Concordia, 1963.

Mackintosh, Robert. *Historic Theories of Atonement.* New York: Hodder and Stoughton, 1920.

Marsden, George. *Jonathan Edwards: A Life.* New Haven, CT: Yale University Press, 2003.

McClymond, Michael J., and Gerald R. McDermott. *The Theology of Jonathan Edwards.* Oxford: Oxford University Press, 2012.

McDonald, H. D. *The Atonement of the Death of Christ: In Faith, Revelation, and History.* Grand Rapids: Baker, 1985.

McMullen, Michael D., ed. *The Glory and Honor of God: Previously Unpublished Sermons of Jonathan Edwards.* Vol. 2. Nashville: Broadman and Holman, 2004.

Melanchthon, Philip. *Melanchthon on Christian Doctrine: Loci Communes, 1555.* Edited and translated by Clyde L. Manschreck. Grand Rapids: Baker, 1965.

Mozley, J. K. *The Doctrine of the Atonement.* London: Duckworth, 1915.

Muller, Richard. *God, Creation, and Providence in the Thought of Jacob Arminius: Sources and Directions of Scholastic Protestantism in the Era of Early Orthodoxy.* Grand Rapids: Baker, 1991.

Murray, Iain. *Jonathan Edwards: A New Biography.* Carlisle, PA: Banner of Truth Trust, 1987.

Noll, Mark A. "Edwards, Jonathan." In *The Blackwell Encyclopedia of Modern Christian Thought,* edited by Alister McGrath, 146. Cambridge, MA: Blackwell, 1993.

Bibliography

———. "Jonathan Edwards, Moral Philosophy, and the Secularization of American Christian Thought." *Reformed Journal* 33 (February 1983) 22–28.

———. *The Scandal of the Evangelical Mind.* Grand Rapids: Eerdmans, 1994.

Olson, Mark Jeffrey. *Irenaeus, the Valentinian Gnostics, and the Kingdom of God: The Debate about 1 Corinthians 15:50.* Lewiston, NY: E. Mellen, 1992.

Owen, John. *The Death of Death in the Death of Christ.* Reprint ed. Carlisle, PA: Banner of Truth Trust, 2002.

———. *The Works of John Owen.* Vol. 10. Edited by William H. Goold. Carlisle, PA: Banner of Truth Trust, 2000.

Packer, J. I. "The Glory of God and the Reviving of Religion: A Study in the Mind of Jonathan Edwards." In *A God Entranced Vision of All Things: The Legacy of Jonathan Edwards,* edited by John Piper and Justin Taylor, 81–108. Wheaton, IL: Crossway, 2004.

———. *A Quest for Godliness: The Puritan Vision of the Christian Life.* Wheaton, IL: Crossway, 1990.

———. *The Redemption and Restoration of Man in the Thought of Richard Baxter.* Vancouver: Regent College Publishing, 2003.

———. "What Did the Cross Achieve?: The Logic of Penal Substitution." *Tyndale Bulletin* 25 (1974) 3–45.

Park, Edwards Amasa. *The Atonement: Discourses and Treatises by Edwards, Smalley, Maxcy, Emmons, Griffin, Burge, and Weeks.* Boston: Congregational Board of Publication, 1859.

Pelikan, Jaroslav. *The Christian Tradition: A History of the Development of Doctrine.* 5 vols. Chicago: University of Chicago Press, 1975–91.

Peterson, Robert A. *Calvin's Doctrine of the Atonement.* Phillipsburg, NJ: Presbyterian and Reformed, 1983.

Pinson, J. Matthew. "The Nature of Atonement in the Theology of Jacobus Arminius." *Journal of the Evangelical Theological Society* 53:4 (December 2010) 773–85.

Piper, John. *God's Passion for His Glory: Living the Vision of Jonathan Edwards.* Wheaton, IL: Crossway, 1998.

Reymond, Robert. *A New Systematic Theology of the Christian Faith.* Nashville: T. Nelson, 1998.

Roberts, Alexander, and James Donaldson, eds. *Ante-Nicene Fathers.* Vols. 1–2. Peabody, MA: Hendrickson, 1995.

Rudisill, Dorus Paul. *The Doctrine of the Atonement in Jonathan Edwards and His Successors.* New York: Poseidon, 1971.

Schaff, Phillip, ed. *The Creeds of Christendom.* Vol. 3: *The Evangelical Protestant Creeds.* Grand Rapids: Baker, 1998.

Schaff, Phillip, and Henry Wace, eds. *The Nicene and Post-Nicene Fathers.* Vol. 5. Edinburgh: T. & T. Clark, 1994.

Schwartz, Benjamin. "New and Noteworthy: What to Read This Month." *The Atlantic,* April 2003, 91–92.

Spitz, Lewis W., ed. *The Reformation: Basic Interpretations.* Lexington, MA: D. C. Heath, 1962.

Stephens, W. P. *The Theology of Huldrych Zwingli.* Oxford: Oxford University Press, 1986.

Strachan, Owen, and Douglas A. Sweeney. *Jonathan Edwards on Beauty.* Chicago: Moody, 2010.

Bibliography

Sweeney, Douglas A., and Allen C. Guelzo, eds. *The New England Theology: From Jonathan Edwards to Edwards Amasa Park*. Grand Rapids: Baker Academic, 2006.

Townsend, Harvey. *The Philosophy of Jonathan Edwards*. Westport, CT: Greenwood, 1955.

Turretin, Francis. *The Atonement of Christ*. Translated by James R. Wilson. Grand Rapids: Baker, 1978.

———. *Institutes of Elenctic Theology*. Vol. 2. Edited by James T. Dennison Jr., translated by George Musgrave Giger. Phillipsburg, NJ: P & R, 1994.

Valeri, Mark. *Law and Providence in Joseph Bellamy's New England*. Oxford: Oxford University Press, 1994.

Vidu, Adonis. *Atonement, Law, and Justice: The Cross in Historical and Cultural Contexts*. Grand Rapids: Baker Academic, 2014.

Wallace, Ronald. *The Atoning Death of Christ*. Wheaton, IL: Crossway, 1981.

Warch, Richard. *School of the Prophets: Yale College, 1701–1740*. New Haven, CT: Yale University Press, 1973.

Warfield, Benjamin Breckinridge. *Studies in Theology*. New York: Oxford University Press, 1932.

West, Stephen. *The Scripture Doctrine of Atonement: Proposed to Careful Examination*. London: Forgotten Books, 2015.

Yeager, Jonathan M., ed. *Early Evangelicalism: A Reader*. Oxford: Oxford University Press, 2013.

Zwingli, Ulrich. *Works of Zwingli*. Vol. 2. Edited by William John Hinke, translated by the American Society of Church History. Philadelphia: Heidelberg, 1922.

———. *Works of Zwingli*. Vol. 3. Edited by Clarence Nevin Heller, translated by the American Society of Church History. Philadelphia: Heidelberg, 1929

www.ingramcontent.com/pod-product-compliance
Lightning Source LLC
Chambersburg PA
CBHW071508150426
43191CB00009B/1447